First published 1991
Lloyd Cole
37 College Avenue
Maidenhead, SL6 6AZ, UK

ISBN 1 874052 05 0

British Library Cataloguing in Publication Data
is available from the British Library

Produced by Chase Production Services,
Chipping Norton, Oxon, OX7 5QR
Printed in Finland

SUCCESSFUL SELLING

Lloyd Cole

The 'Successful' Series

1991

Lloyd Cole

Maidenhead

CONTENTS

PART 1 RETAIL SELLING

CONTENTS

PART 2 SELLING TO THE RETAIL TRADE

PART 1

RETAIL SELLING

INTRODUCTION

'England is a nation of shopkeepers.'
Napoleon

A statement of this sort is one which may or may not be true in relation to a particular case. It may be regarded as a compliment or just the opposite.

It is beyond dispute that England has always had plenty of shops, perhaps too many. Some must fail. Perhaps there will not be enough business to go round. Failure is likely among those who have entered a business for which they are not suited or who have undertaken an enterprise without sufficient capital. Some lack staying power and others lack enterprise. Businesses do not fail through no fault of the owners. If you fail it is likely to be your fault.

The list of bankruptcies is increasing, as is what might be called commercial dishonesty. This should make newcomers to trade very cautious in considering the prospects of success before commencement. Today, the fashion for walk-about precincts leaves room only for multiples and the like who can afford the huge rents asked. The small man is slowly being squeezed out in these circumstances. Only the best will be able to compete with the large stores and supermarkets. The small shopkeeper must be fully equipped for the enterprise undertaken.

However, this nation of shopkeepers has outlasted the tormentor. A good shopkeeper has nothing to be ashamed of. Success in any form of business is a victory over opposition and circumstances, and is an achievement to be proud of. Happiness comes to those who give happiness and success to those who deserve success. To create something out of nothing or to improve on something already existing is rewarding. A nation of shop-keepers may well be a very contented nation.

To say that someone who failed had worked so hard he deserved to be a success is a false assertion. It is nonsense. Success comes to those who deserve it. It is possible to work hard in the wrong way and fail. A shop may take £5000 per day and not make a profit. You can sell more bananas than anyone else in town and be losing money because you sell too cheaply or to people who do not pay, or because you bought at the wrong price. It is easy to sell at a loss or to people who do not pay.

With regard to success, as in all other forms of business, success is measured in net profit and not in turnover. High turnover can occur hand in hand with low profit or actual loss. No one should start in business unless fully understanding the basic principles on which a successful business can be built.The parable of the two houses is well known, one built on rock and one on sand. When the storms came the one was swept away while the other remained firmly rooted on its rockbase. The house built on sand looked well while the weather was calm, just as a badly based business will look fine while conditions for trade are helpful, but will collapse under pressure. Did the man who built on sand deserve to succeed because he worked so hard? Of course not. Remember that in trade there are storms and winds of ill fortune. There are strikes, recessions, lack of work, bad weather, change of circumstances, etc. Only the soundly based will survive.

In the pages that follow we must discuss the trade to suit your talents and finance, and the right location for success. The kind of person you and your staff should be, and the finance needed. We will consider buying, stock control, display, advertising and so on.

It will be observed that a businessman should not be only a businessman. He should lead a balanced life, finding happiness as well as success.

This book contains notes of experiences in business and notes of things said and read about business – all to help the newcomer to become a success.

INTRODUCTION

You will notice that I refer to the business*man* which is not to say that I am excluding women – there are many successful business women in the retail trade, some of whom have made it to the very top like Anita Roddick of The Body Shop. It is just that I will be using the male gender for ease of readability and everything I say applies equally to women.

1

WHAT DO YOU WANT?

Misfits cannot expect to be successes. You must enter a business which will suit *you*. Your personality must be right for the trade you enter. You must be able to divide your time between your work and social and other interests as you would wish. You must understand, when entering a trade, exactly what sacrifices will be called for in loss of time for other interests. Otherwise you may find that the business will be neglected and will therefore fail. Alternatively, family or others will suffer because all your time is taken up with business.

If in taking up a retail business you are going to invest your savings or mortgage your home to raise the necessary capital, it is surely advisable to make sure you enter the appropriate business for you. You may buy an existing business or start from scratch. Whichever it is make sure it is going to be the kind of business you are going to enjoy and one leaving you time for any other interests you want to maintain. The hours you need to work are an important factor.

If you are going to do all the work yourself or you and your wife are going to do all between you make sure the hours and amount of work suit you. Do not buy a newsagent's shop if you dislike getting up early in the morning. With many businesses it is necessary to open through the lunch hour, with others it is essential to open at the weekend. In a business located at the coast Sunday trade could be more than half the trade for the week. It would be ridiculous to have a business in a position for super Sunday sales and not take advantage of it.

What do you want? You want to make money of course, but how much do you wish to sacrifice to this end? Consider that it is not worthwhile to make money at the cost of losing your health. The richest man in the cemetery is not much to be admired. An overworked and harassed man is of little use to his family.

What do you want? Most people want enough plus a little so as to be able to enjoy life to the full. You may have to sacrifice much to obtain this position but remember the value of a loving wife and children. Do not forget them in the search for gold. Some time you must enjoy the quiet life. There will still be time for ambition which is a good thing, and enthusiasm is the life and soul of a business. One of my customers in the past asked how I managed to be so enthusiastic about the goods I was selling. He said that quite often he bought what he did not need because of my lively enjoyment of what I was doing. Nothing worthwhile is achieved without enthusiasm. Be enthusiastic while remembering that *personal happiness is every bit as important as personal fortune.*

What do you want? You want to be your own boss – a very worthwhile aim.

However, there is little to being your own boss if you only lose the money you saved while working for others. A business is useless if the profits amount to less than you could earn working for someone else.

Many of Napoleon's shopkeepers lose all they had or work for less than they could have earned at their old jobs. A wish for freedom and a desire for profit keep the world turning. To attain freedom with good profits is success. Freedom to starve is worthless.

Profit comes from building up a business on sound principles. Good businesses are founded by men of integrity.

What do you want? If you only want to work certain hours or days choose a business which will allow for this. *You are more likely to succeed doing what you want to do.* If you want to be able to leave the running of your business in the main to others choose a business which will become big enough to allow for this. If you want a business which you and your wife can run choose a business which will show enough profit without you killing yourself. A lot depends on one's view of life – what suits one man will kill another. Some want long breaks from work. Others will gladly take on more and more work. What do you want? Do what suits you.

Decide what will give you happiness and what your values are. Do not make a mistake in this or you may be unhappy and unsuccessful, or successful at the expense of contentment.

I must labour this point. Human happiness and relationships are of major importance. To lose a loving wife or the respect of your children is failure not success. The great purpose of your life should be happiness not wealth – but you can have both. Just do not pay too high a price for the one, so that you lose the other. You cannot get more out of a business than you put in – the same applies to a relationship. Hit the happy medium and true success is yours. Be on top in business and happy at home. Make that little more than enough without losing friends. Have a *successful life* not just a successful business.

Decide what you want. Then let nothing divert you from your goal. There is no point in leaving a fortune when you die if you never lived. Likewise lukewarmness in business will lead to failure. You can enjoy life without allowing your ambition to run away with you. You can have business success without losing the love of your loved ones who need your attention and kindness. Take no step into business until you have decided what you want. Decide your values first, now. Then stick to them.

The foregoing has shown that it is better to enter a trade *you know something about*. The chances of success are greater if one deals in goods of which one has at least some knowledge. Knowing something about the goods you intend buying will protect you against unscrupulous and dishonest suppliers and salesmen. Try to attain a basic knowledge of values in the trade concerned and get an idea of present trends. Study trade papers. Observe what successful traders are showing. Note also items which do not appear to be selling. Work out why one shop is successful and another not so. Study goods on offer; study other traders attitudes to customers; study prices, display and advertising done. Compare the successful with the failures and learn. Concentrate on what is good to do and buy. *Knowledge is power.* Know all you can before you start. Learning by experience can be very expensive.

Look around in the area in which you intend to open your shop and make sure your trade is not fully catered for. If much is already on offer think out why you should succeed. Can you offer better selection or lower prices? Can you give more cheerful and pleasant service? Can you make your shop look more modern and more interesting? Do not open up in opposition to established traders if you have nothing extra to offer. Be sure you have an edge. If there are many already trading this means there is plenty of business. What matters is who is going to get it.

In a Midlands town there were several shops selling lingerie, handbags and jewellery. However all the shops were old and the owners rather smug and settled in their ways. Along came an enterprising young lady who opened a boutique offering the same items as were abundantly provided already. In a short time she had the business from her competitors, and was the most successful in her lines within a year of opening. Why? It was not price as she sold dearer. The secret was *difference*. She put a ship's wheel in her window and draped it with lingerie and jewellery. She put two big coach lamps outside the shop. She let light into the shop. She had the new colours and fashions *first*. Her shop looked different, more tempting.

Ideas will beat the humdrum every day. A light interesting shop will outsell the old fashioned dingy shop, even if the latter has been there 100 years.

When considering whether a trade is catered for in your area, think whether it is catered for at all price levels. If everyone is cheap, be expensive and if all are expensive open at cut price level. If the existing traders believe that nothing will sell over a certain price you can set about supplying the more exclusive. You will hear that everyone goes to the nearby bigger town for this and that – *stop them*. If you can establish a business for better-class merchandise you can obtain more exclusive lines. You are unlikely to get sole rights in your area for very cheap items, but you might well do so for higher priced goods.

If others are dabbling with this or that do the job properly with a wide selection of each line. Offer the best choice in the town. *The man who dabbles will never harm the man who specialises*. No trade is catered for until it is fully catered for. Have the best selection in town. If you have the best selection you can get the best price.

If, on the other hand, everybody is expensive go the other way. Instead of the exclusive, present the bargain. Open an 'economy' or 'cut-price' shop. Having said this, I tend to think that it is likely to be more profitable to raise the tone of a trade rather than lower it. You will never be able to fight the super-markets on price, but you can on quality and service.

Try to avoid being caught up in a price war. It is very easy to attain a high turnover at a loss. Offer good and courteous service. Display well. Use space and light. Choose a trade in which supplies are available on the best terms to small traders. It might be best to avoid those lines which are sold at much lower prices to supermarkets.

To summarise what has been said in this chapter:

- Choose a trade that suits your personality and what you want out of life.

- Choose a business you can run yourself if that is what you want to do.

- If you want to employ staff to do most of the work start a business with sufficient potential.

- Do not allow business life to cancel private life.

- Make sure you will earn more in profit than you could earn in wages.

- Know well that success has to be earned.

- Be reliable.

- Have integrity.

- Do what you want to do.

- Know something about what you do.

- Study the successful and the failures and learn.

- Find out how far your trade is catered for and be different.

- Be original, be light and bright.

- Deal in goods obtainable at the best prices.

THE IMPORTANCE OF POSITION

Position is Half the Battle

Of the many things to consider concerning starting a new business, position is paramount. A business can fail by being on the wrong side of the street, or by being where cars cannot park, or by looking less inviting than other shops. Choose position carefully. A higher rent or purchase price may be redeemed by a greater turnover resulting. A low rent may mean poor sales. Everything is relative. Remember a good position in a failing community is not as good as the same position in an up and coming and progressive town.

It may pay to buy an existing business to get the best position.

A considerable opportunity is provided by the many new estates around existing towns. Such are close to the public who use them, have car parks, and more reasonable rents than town centres.

On estates you know who your customers are and what you have to cater for, and many people have made a great success out of establishing themselves on one of the new housing developments.

Beware of the mistake of not holding a wide stock on the grounds that the absence of a passing public makes this unnecessary. The opposite is true. Lacking a passing public, it is all the more important to stock the widest choice available. You keep customers by giving the best service. When a supermarket opens on an estate the range offered is as wide as in the town centre.

Do not sacrifice the advantage of a good position by a disinterested attitude to customers, or by gloomy, unimaginative window display.

Back Position with Panache.

To summarise:

- Get the best position you can.

- Pay a higher purchase price or rent if necessary.

- Consider new estates, on which you should offer as good a selection as anyone in the town centre.

DISCOUNTS ARE PROFITS

Never Owe a Penny You Do Not Need to Owe

I have been struck by the pride and happiness of many retailers who have said to me, 'we've only been open a short time, but all the stock is paid for, and we settle all our accounts in seven days for discounts.'

Bad debts are on the increase. Therefore the prompt payer has the opportunity to obtain the best goods at the best prices. The wise and successful manufacturer is getting more and more careful as to whom he gives credit and how much.

Many manufacturers and wholesalers have been forced out of business by bad debts. This means that the best suppliers will not supply you if your credit rating is poor. This means you will have to sell the second best or worse because you cannot get the best.

On commencing a new business one should have enough capital in hand to cover at least three months purchases and as the business grows this position should at least be maintained. If you think about it, why should someone else finance your business? The road to success in business is to buy only the best on the best possible terms. *The prompt payer gets prompt supplies.* He gets supplies when items are in short supply. When a maker has more orders than supplies he will supply the prompt payer first. You see, if items are in short supply, your supplier will get more if he pays promptly, so if you pay him ...!

Prompt payers get discounts. Money talks the loudest, and discounts are profits. Every time you get a better discount you increase your profits. It is said of one American store that they put all the discounts they took into property so that after a number of years the property they owned was worth more than the store. On purchases of £50000 in a year a five percent discount is £2500. This adds nicely to profit. *A bad payer has the worst lines or the best lines on worst terms*. If you did not take discounts on £50000 you lost £2500.

Suppose you want a loan from your bank. Do you see that you are more likely to get it if you have £50000 stock paid for than if you owe £50000. If you have used your capital to pay for your stock and need money for a special purpose you will probably get it. If you have stock not paid for and need a loan to hold off the creditors you may not get it. Prompt payment is important to suppliers. Big orders with no certainty of payment are easily obtainable. It is becoming harder from day to day to obtain prompt payment. If you pay promptly the best suppliers want you.

You want to buy direct. Then you must pay promptly. Otherwise your supplies will have to come from middlemen who charge more. Not only do you lose discounts but you pay more for the goods as well. You must see that slow payment means smaller profits.

A reasonable turnover for a small shop is £100000. Without discounts the shopkeeper makes about £5000 less. This could be the difference between success and insolvency. A retailer making less in this way is tempted to cut prices to get money in quickly, so he makes even less, and his profit may not be covering his overheads. Therefore do not start trading unless you can buy at the best terms in the trade. Trade at first within your capability to pay promptly. Overtrading means that you are trying to do too much business with the money you have available. In this position a small recession will cause disaster. If your capital is limited do not try to spread it too far.

Do not boast of the amount of stock you have unless it is paid for. *Until it is paid for it is not yours.*

A word of caution. When buying for cash, only sell for cash unless you have large reserves of capital. It is stupid to be in a position of not being able to pay your accounts because you have not been paid.

Good accountancy advice is to prepare a budget. Work out expected turnover, the cost of the goods needed, and all expenses including living expenses. If capital available is not sufficient cut the intended turnover down. This will reduce the amount needed for buying but not the running expenses. Work to reach a balance between money available and trade to be done. Be satisfied. Plough profits back into the business as far as you can. This will increase capital available. You can then increase intended sales. Progress may not be spectacular but it will be soundly based. Money available is the springboard for action. Expand too fast and you finish up with nothing. Hard work will not make you successful.

To summarise:

- Have capital for three month's trading.

- Pay promptly.

- Take discounts.

- Work to a budget.

4

FRIENDLINESS IS GOLDEN

Other things being equal *you will always sell more to someone you like and who likes you*. Friendliness is often in short supply in the modern business world, yet it is always highly valued when offered. Samuel Johnson said that friendliness was the wine of life and each man should keep a well-stocked cellar. Most shoppers will respond to a friendly shopkeeper and wish to spend their money in that shop. A friendly attitude that springs from a real liking for people is a great asset. Customers should be made welcome, otherwise why should they enter your shop. There are shops and hotels which I would never enter a second time. I will not spend my hard-earned money with a shopkeeper who displays an off-hand manner or take-it-or-leave-it attitude. Many must feel as I do. Remember it is just as easy to be friendly as unfriendly. In fact it is easier and will be of benefit in health and in business done.

Your shop should be a place customers are delighted to visit. Be easy to talk to, never superior, never too busy to give attention.

Emerson said, 'A friend may be reckoned the masterpiece of nature.' Nobody can have too many friends. People who cannot make friends should not be retailers. Behind the counter you will have many chances to make friends. Study to be liked. Many people have a hard life and appreciate friendliness. Your friendship should not be calculated but natural. Remember happiness comes to those who spread happiness. People prefer to deal with those they like, and feel at ease with.

Be friendly though, not smarmy or smart. In addition to friendliness, cultivate honesty. The smart alec may seem to succeed but the enduring success goes to the retailer with integrity. The average customer will return to a friendly and honest dealer. Let your attitude be one of friendliness, and your actions those of an honest man. You will get loyalty and friendliness in return.

Be truthful. Do not employ lies to sell your goods. You may sell one item now and lose sales for long after.

Your attitude to salesmen who call to sell to you is also important. The idea that the buyer is God and the salesman there to suit his every whim is ridiculously outdated. I spent a good deal of time selling to retailers, and the following may illustrate points I wish to make.

I called one day on a retailer who asked, 'Who do you represent?'

'So and So,' I replied.

'Never heard of them,' he said in a superior tone, as though there was a smell under his nose.

This upset me and I said, 'Well, I never heard of you until today.' This lead to an argument during which I said that he (the buyer) could not possibly know everything, and that possibly someone, somewhere, might at some time produce goods which would be of interest to him, and yet he would not know about it. I pointed out that I was the link between the supplier and himself without which he might find his shop window empty.

There is absolutely no justification for superior or rude behaviour to salesmen. Also no retailer can afford to make enemies of salesmen who call on him. He should show the courtesy he expects in return. I well remember calling on another retailer who was extremely off-hand and rude in his attitude. I therefore put my goods in a shop opposite to him. He later wrote to my firm asking to have our goods. I called and reminded him that he had treated me so badly. He apologised now that it suited him and said that my firm ought to supply him as his was the best shop in town for our goods, and he the most successful in selling such goods. I said it was a pity, if he was such a good businessman, that he did not act like one. I told him I had no faith in rude and overbearing people, and that I would prefer to deal with the very nice and courteous people with whom I had opened an account at the time of his original inability to behave like a gentleman. My new customer soon took most of the trade away from this overbearing and self-satisfied example of pomposity, until, eventually, he was forced to drop the line from his range of goods altogether.

On another occasion I had called on a retailer by appointment and was showing the buyer my merchandise. Into the shop came a car salesman from the local garage to discuss with the lady buyer the purchase of a new car. She asked to be excused to talk to this car salesman. After over half an hour she returned to me and said, 'I will not have time to see you now.'

I said, 'Madam, I did have an appointment with you, and I have been here for some time.'

She replied, 'Oh, that's one of the things you chaps have to put up with.'

I said, 'I am afraid you are mistaken madam. If you do not see me now, you will certainly not see me again. I refuse to be treated in this way, and if you really intend to refuse to see my range now, I shall open another account, and I will work hard to make sure that I get a window full of our products as near to you as possible.'

This I did, and as my lines were the best in the trade in question, this lady lost a great deal of future business through thinking that only *her* time was important. The salesman's time is important too. Often more important. Remember, the man who calls to sell to you may be worth ten times what you are worth. His time is then worth ten times what your time is worth. If you waste half his morning and then refuse to finish looking at his range, you have probably made it impossible for him to do any other business that morning, especially if his nearest call is some way away. If you treat the best salesmen in this way you will be left with only the second-best to call on you, and you will have only the second-best goods on your shelf – and serve you right.

A top salesman with a good range of merchandise probably earns many times what the buyers he calls on can earn. Such buyers have little if any justification for a smug attitude.

Be courteous to salesmen and you will benefit. It costs little to behave in a gentlemanly manner, but it can bring considerable reward. When selling, I always looked after the decent people among my customers. Those who wasted my time once never did so again. Behave to someone selling to you as you would wish your customers to behave when you are selling to them.

A further asset the retailer needs is faith in the goods he sells. *If you do not believe in what you are selling why should anyone else.*

To summarise:

• Be friendly, honest, truthful and courteous.

5

BUY TO LEAD

Buy Badly – Sell Slowly. There is much truth in that statement. The success of any retail business depends very much on good buying. To buy correctly and to the best advantage it is necessary to know who to buy from. One guiding rule should be observed: if you can, *buy from specialists only*. Do not buy toys from a firm that sell a few as a sideline. Buy toys from a firm that specialises in toys. Do not buy costume jewellery from a toy merchant who sells a few lines only. Buy only from experts in the trade concerned. Buy from manufacturers or direct importers who can offer you the pick from all over the world.

If you buy sidelines you will never have the right lines or the right price. Would you buy a suit from a hairdresser? Or would you go to a well-known tailor? It is sometimes better not to buy from very local firms so that you do not have exactly the same goods as everybody else in the district.

Price is important in buying, but there are other considerations as well. Importance must be attached to dependable delivery, wide choice, latest lines being available, unusual and interesting lines.

For dependability the small wholesaler may not be suitable. Perhaps he only buys hand-to-mouth and does not hold good stocks. In which case he cannot deliver repeat orders quickly. Deal with a big and strong firm holding large stocks.

For wide choice the same applies. Some retailers buy from wholesaler A today, but when seeing wholesaler B the next day feel they would not have bought from A if they had known what was on offer from B. Better to buy from a company with a wide range. It is absolute folly to buy bits here and there and never to see the whole availability at one firm.

Consider the latest fashion lines. These may not be available from the small wholesaler who restricts himself to regular and usual selling lines. From the specialist firm you can buy all the usual lines plus many unusual and exclusive lines the small man would not be offering.

Today and in the future the successful retailer is going to be the specialist with unusual and exclusive merchandise to offer. A move in this direction will ensure a retailer's future.

The best bet today for any retailer is specialisation. Be the best shop in town for this or that. Many boutiques are proving this policy to be successful.

Once the new retailer has decided where to buy he must consider what to buy. A mistake many make is to buy only what they like. This can be fatal. It can never be true that all your customers will like things you like. Some will and some will not. You need a wide selection to suit a widely differing range of tastes. Cater for all tastes. *Lead rather than follow fashion.* Be first with the latest.

The retailer looking at a new line who says, 'I'll buy it if I'm asked for it' is unlikely to be asked for anything. His customers will have bought the line elsewhere from a shop-keeper who anticipated the demand. A wide range of goods will draw a wide public. The retailer who will survive is ahead of fashion, anticipating trends, with a window display of the best plus something unusual or unique. You certainly cannot sell it if it is not there.

A first-class, large, well-established company with a national advertising programme, will not mislead a customer, and advice can be taken from their representatives as to best sellers in their range. Such good suppliers build their business on good relationships with their customers. To buy safely, buy from companies who would not tolerate any unjust treatment of a customer. Advice given by such companies can be worth a great deal.

Good advice will steer you away from buying only what you like. Narrowing your sales to those who have the same likes as yourself is the supreme stupidity. Another error to avoid is that of buying the same lines for ever and ever. Success comes from *distinguishing between lines which have a universal appeal for almost all time, and those which sell in larger quantities but only for a short time.*

Beware of convincing yourself that certain things will not sell in your area. Most good sellers sell everywhere. If you say that such a line might sell in X but not in your shop no doubt your customers will go to X to get it.

A shopkeeper may say, 'We don't get teenagers in here.' No wonder – there is nothing to appeal to them. Of course they go to the next town to get what they want. If you persuade yourself that you are in the wrong town then you probably are. If you keep saying this and that will not sell in your shop it is possible that you are also in the wrong business. Be positive. Find out what people go to X to buy and stock it. It is best not to talk yourself into bankruptcy. After all, why do you think your town is so bad? Surely there are people. Do the super- markets close down for lack of business? Are there no children born there and no teenagers looking for the new and inter- esting? Are you not as good a shopkeeper as those in X? Perhaps your personal prejudices are stronger than your business ability. Faint heart never won large turnover!

A further word about treatment of salesmen calling to sell to you. It is important to know what is available. Do not be too busy to look at ranges of goods offered to you. *The buyer who is always too busy to buy will probably be too late to sell.*

Do not think you know everything. Do not believe that you have all the suppliers you need. Do not believe that nobody could sell the same lines to you at a lower price. How do you know if you do not look? For heavens sake, *look*. It is the buyer's job to know what is new. It is the buyer's job to know what is selling. It is the buyer's job to be always looking for better suppliers. Make time to look at all goods from worth- while companies. Do not say 'We are not opening any new accounts' – this is an absurdity coming from a buyer. *Look* and be sure whether or not you want the lines on offer.

Don't refuse a new supplier without consideration any more than you would refuse a new customer. After all, the customer is dealing with a new supplier when first he buys from you.

The most successful are the best informed. You may find yourself saying 'Where can I get so and so?' Perhaps you refused to see the very salesman who wanted to offer it to you. Be in the know.

The retailer must know many sources of supply. He should

know who is best for price and for prompt delivery. He must know where to find the unusual in his trade. All information which can improve his business must be sought and retained by the retailer who wants to build a good business. Every trade paper, every exhibition, every salesman is an opportunity to improve one's trade. *If you are too busy to learn you may be busy getting nowhere.*

One thing to remember when buying is that cost price is not selling price. A line may seem good at the price offered to you but will it seem good when you have added your profit margin? *The price that matters is the price you sell at.* When looking at a salesman's range look at the whole range before buying anything, otherwise you may buy the least suitable.

Consider carefully the trading terms offered by suppliers. What level of credit can you get? What discounts can you get? Do you pay carriage? Are unsold goods returnable? Will damaged or broken items be replaced free of charge? What point-of-sale aids are offered? Are there discounts for quantity? Can you get sole rights in the area? Do not be forced to buy too large a quantity of anything. When both parties to a deal are being reasonable a basis for trading will be found. Know how much you spend.

In fashion trade be a leader. Do not always be running behind somebody else or when you catch up with what they are doing they will be moving on to something else. Do not forget that a shop gets known. You decide what your shop will be known for. The latest or the dated. A wide range or odds and ends. A shopkeeper gets the trade he deserves.

Apart from the grocery trade the small shop has little to fear from stores. Specialise. Show the best range in something and buyers will come to you. Be unusual and exclusive for something. Make your shop bright and attractive. Take care with what you buy and how you show it. Take an interest in your customers. Buy well. *Nothing is cheap if you cannot sell it.* Remember *any fool can buy rubbish cheap.* Remember success is net profit.

To summarise:

- Buy from specialists.

- Buy from well-established companies.
- Remember price is not the only thing to think of.
- Consider variety of goods offered, and how early new fashions are offered.
- Note if good stocks kept to meet repeat orders.
- Specialise yourself.
- Buy a wide range, not only what you like yourself.
- Believe in your area for your business.
- Best sellers are best sellers because they sell everywhere.
- Do not be too busy to buy properly.
- Learn all the time.
- See every salesman you can, read trade papers, attend exhibitions.
- When buying consider the selling price.
- Buying cheap rubbish is no great achievement.
- Success comes to those who deserve it.

6

SPECIALISE AND PROSPER

Let us think further about specialisation which is the watchword for modern retailing. The retailer has to succeed in the face of many stores and supermarkets. This surely points to the need for specialisation by the small man. Not only so, but preferably specialisation in those lines not much in evidence in supermarkets. The general shop is dead except in very small places. The modern boutique is flourishing. Some very successful shops sell only greeting cards. Others specialise in costume jewellery or glass. I saw one shop only selling anything that featured a cat – cards, brooches, ornaments, etc.

Shoe shops also do well; as do specialists in tools. Hat shops and dress shops have their place. In fact, all specialist shops are doing well. A really super camera shop would pay in most areas, especially if manned by a good photographer giving advice. Learn all you can about one line and then sell it in as many varieties as you can find. A wide range attracts a wide public. As a specialist you may well obtain sole rights in your district. Specialise and find prosperity.

Once you have the lines show them well. Keep the stock looking bright and clean. Stock in stores and supermarkets is kept fresh looking. Dirty stock destroys customer confidence.

In display, marry lines together which could sell together.

Make sure all your stock is visible. You will not sell items which cannot be seen.

I think it important that stock should all be priced and all items in window display should show a price clearly. I will not enter a shop with unpriced lines in the window. Why should I?

In your town you must become the name that springs to mind when certain articles are being discussed or are needed. This is true specialisation.

In your shop you must know what stock you have, and what sells well and what is hopeless. Without this knowledge it will be very difficult not to become overstocked. You must keep stock under control. You must know the lines you do not need more of – but good lines must be kept in stock.

The above says:

- *Specialise.*
- Keep stock visible and clean.
- Show what you have.
- Price everything.
- Know your stock.

7

SHOW TO SELL

If you show it, you will sell it. If you take the trouble to show it well, you will sell it well.

Modern stores and supermarkets are masters of display, and people get used to this. The small shopkeeper must display well to compete.

The successful shopkeeper is the one who learns from new ideas on marketing, who changes as conditions demand. Such will survive in difficult times. This is to say that the competent survive. Why should fools survive? The lazy have no right to a living.

The small shopkeeper is at the heart of private enterprise. If efficient he will remain in business. It is perfectly natural for the inefficient to perish. The fit survive. The man with the money is the one who decides where he will spend the money. The shopkeeper must influence him to spend his money in his shop. An untidy shop is unfit to meet today's challenges. Clutter obscures what is on offer.

Good display is not necessarily a matter of money. I know of retailers who have made excellent displays of their goods using logs of wood and coloured papers. An enterprising man will find a way to show his goods to advantage even if very little money is available for display stands, etc. I have sold costume jewellery to many shops who have never made the most of the goods they bought. One put a range of rings on the floor base of the window – because the stones are heavier than the shank most of the rings finished up in positions that made it impossible to see the stones in the rings. You will not sell items you do not show properly. Perhaps this retailer could not afford expensive ring stands or pads. What was to stop him winding some coloured paper around a piece of cane or a slender tree branch, and showing the rings on this? Bracelets can also be displayed on a similar arrangement. In almost all trades, effective display pieces can be made at low cost.

However it is done, *it must be done*. Goods must be shown to advantage. In buying, if you buy from efficient and successful suppliers you will often be provided with free display stands. Not only must you have the best lines but it must be seen that you have them.

If your shop is small, why try to sell twice as many lines as you have room for? To sell everything from a pin to an elephant does not necessarily increase turnover. If you sell a wide range of a few lines your display problems are fewer. Lots of good suppliers will provide display aids. Deal with them. Have light, lots of light – and from the biggest window possible so that would-be customers can see in. Then have room to move, with all goods well displayed, and priced.

Instead of the costly way of learning from experience, learn from the experience and practice of others. Learn from the successful. Change your window display as often as you can. Do not cram the window with goods.

So ...

- Show your goods to best advantage.

- Make your shop light and roomy.

- Consider all-glass doors to show interior.

- Change display often.

8

NET PROFIT MATTERS

Turnover, in itself, does not mean success. You can sell a lot at a loss. A big turnover is no good unless it means a good measure of net profit. If you sell an item at a penny loss, the more you sell, the greater the loss. To sell at a penny profit is good and the more you sell the better.

You really only earn when the money you take gives a profit big enough to more than meet all your expenses.

In a small shop you will only sell small quantities compared with a supermarket. Therefore keep away from the lines supermarkets sell ... and specialise. If you can sell exclusive specialities *at a higher price* you will earn the same profit for less work.

Therefore you have only one thing to remember – you need net profit.

• Turnover alone, however large, may only mean losses.

9

INTELLIGENT ADVERTISING

The well known adage 'It pays to Advertise' is in most cases correct, but there are circumstances in which it does not pay to advertise. Perhaps we can amend the adage to say: *'It always pays to advertise the right goods at the right time in the right place'*. I imagine the total amount of money wasted on useless advertising would completely wipe out the national debt. Yet, all advertising pays when it is intelligent.

Remember that advertising for the small business is not the same as advertising for Cadburys for example. The time to advertise is important – why advertise cricket bats at the start of the football season?

There is no point in advertising to thousands of people who will never come near your shop. Before advertising in any medium consider not only the size of its circulation but where it circulates. Small circulation media are of little use. However large circulations serve little purpose if the larger part of that circulation is to people who would never come to your shop. The cost would be out of proportion to the results achieved. Therefore not only is the size of circulation of a medium important but it must be the right circulation for you.

Of local advertising, let us sort out the useful from the useless. Church magazines are of very little use. You can advertise in them as a charitable gesture but do not expect much business to result. Churches have never been emptier. It would be better to have the shop painted or buy some new display units than to waste money on this form of advertising.

Yellow Pages is quite a useful medium for local advertising although there is considerable wastage as the circulation of each directory covers a wide area – too wide for many local shops.

However, there is also the point that suppliers read *Yellow Pages* when looking for possible buyers. This may serve you well. It may be said however that the inclusion of your name in the directories (which is free) may be enough. If there are likely to be traders with the same name, then a bold type entry might be worthwhile to help customers and suppliers to seek you out.

Local and county guide books are not usually a very good medium. There is little guaranteed circulation. Such guides are often given away or sold on sale-or-return to outlets. Because the circulation is small and suspect the publisher makes his profit from the advertising booked. The advertisers are the losers.

The best local advertising medium is the local newspaper. Regular notices in such papers will help to establish a reputation for your shop.

Remember never advertise just to see your name in print, only to produce sales. If at all possible, local advertising should coincide with national advertising by the manufacturer of the products you sell.

If your shop is in the town centre local newspaper advertising will have little or no wastage as most people in an area visit the town centre. If your shop is on an estate it is likely to be visited only by people living on that estate – advertising in the local paper represents considerable wastage as far as you are concerned.

On estates the best advertising will be that which covers the estate thoroughly. To do this, circulars of all kinds are the best medium. Care must be taken that they are delivered properly. A shopkeeper can make his circular worth something when brought into the shop. This offer can be for a limited time and limited to a discount off certain items if desired. A circular pushes you and your shop only, without the competition of any other advertisers.

Local newspaper advertising should be regular to be effective. Spend your advertising budget carefully in the right medium and regularly. Local advertising should accomplish for you what national advertising accomplishes for the manufacturer. The idea is to achieve locally what the manufacturer wants to achieve nationally. Ideally when a local person thinks of the manufactured item, he thinks of you. To achieve this, advertise regularly. *Say a thing often enough and it will be remembered and believed.*

Having said all the above, the best advertisement will be your shop itself, and the attitude of yourself and your staff. To spend a lot of money on advertising while the shop has not been painted for years and inside gives the impression of an unsuccessful jumble sale, will mean you have wasted your money. On top of this, if staff are indifferent or surly you likewise have advertised to no end.

This brings us back to matters discussed in earlier chapters. Your shop must be light and bright. Make people feel welcome.

The aim of advertising is to produce the best possible results at the minimum cost. Special efforts at Christmas time will do more good than the same effort in January.

In newspaper advertising do not crowd the space you use. You want to gain attention, arouse interest, and finally spur to action. Make your advertisements simple and direct. Make sure your advertisement is put in the right spot in a newspaper. Do not advertise a ladies garment in the horse-racing section. You are spending your money. Make sure you spend it sensibly.

Summarising:

- The right advertising in the right place will bring results.

- Get the message to the people who are likely to come to your shop.

THE IMPORTANCE OF
STAFF ATTITUDES

The subject of the staff in your shop has been discussed before. It will not hurt to emphasise the importance of selecting the right staff. Any shop can be made or ruined by its staff.

As far as possible it will be best for the small trader to serve himself, and for members of his own family to assist. This is not always possible, and many a retailer has lost considerably by having the wrong staff. Not only do the wrong staff lose business but they make other efforts, such as advertising, a waste of money.

Unfortunately, many young people today seem to have little or no ambition and show little interest in learning anything. The young lady who never says 'Sir' and who stands in front of you chewing gum should be allowed to work for your competitors. There are girls whose faces show utter boredom. These types are not for you.

The would-be assistant who asks what she has to do (rather than does she have to work on Saturdays) is a possibility.

Engage the girl who takes an interest in the goods sold. Snap up the one who wants to know if she can earn a commission for sales above a certain point. Take on the one looking for a permanent job. Find the young people who are not empty headed.

Having selected carefully, train well. Be friendly. Show a young person how much cleverer she can be. Reward good work and increased turnover. Cultivate ambition. Try to find assistants who are going to stay with you. Permanence in your staff can be important. Create a happy atmosphere.

Permanent staff are a good advertisement. An unhappy worker is usually a poor worker. Aim at friendliness without indiscipline.

The friendliness between yourself and the staff should be extended to the customers. A friendly atmosphere will help to keep customer loyalty. I will not return to a shop to be served by someone who looks bored to death, and as if there is a bad smell under their nose. Assistants who cannot make friends cannot make sales either. I expect an assistant in a shop I visit to care whether or not I get what I want. If an assistant does not care, why should I? Aim at friendliness not familiarity. I am not anybody's 'duck' or 'dearie'!

Perhaps I am in a minority but when an assistant says to me 'what can I get you dearie?' I feel like saying that first she could get me an assistant who does not call me dearie. 'Sir' and 'Madam' are really the correct address for customers. Correct address can be used in a friendly way avoiding familiarity. Be friendly and businesslike.

In addition to friendly service, *promptness* is also important. People often do not have time to waste. A customer should never be kept waiting while assistants make conversation together. When I am confronted with this, I walk out. In my case, tomorrow will not do. Once when I entered a shop the assistant was reading a novel and did not even register my presence. I spoke only to be told I had made her lose her place in the book. I told her that if she worked for me she would have lost her job.

We seem to be living in a time when enthusiasm and enterprise are non-starters. People are molly-coddled from the womb to the grave, and expect to do as little as possible. Or, they want to do nothing except live on the state, pilfer all they can, and marry and have children they are unable to support. Avoid these people like the plague. Get your own staff from the still enterprising and independent members of society. Possibly, it may be good policy to avoid young people altogether and employ the over forties who seem to me more businesslike and much more honest.

Retailers who try one young girl after another without finding one suitable might well try the thirty five to forty year olds.

Anybody can sell what a customer has come in for. Try, without being pushy, to sell something the customer was not looking for. The assistant who only sells just what she is asked for is not going to be of much use in any business. Assistants must be trained and encouraged to make sales. Incentive bonuses paid on turnover exceeding a certain amount may be useful in promoting further sales.

The good sales person never gives offense. The customer is made to feel that a helpful suggestion has been made, rather than an attempt to foist something onto them.

Goodwill between your staff and yourself and between your staff and your customers is a recipe for success.

To summarise:

- A shop can be made or ruined by its staff.

- Run the business yourself or with family if you can.

- Do not employ the bored, disinterested and impolite.

- Select carefully.

- Train well, with friendliness.

- Try to keep the same staff.

- Make customers feel welcome.

11

PARTNERSHIPS AND COMPANIES

It used to be necessary for sole traders and partnerships to register their business name but this was changed in The Companies Act, 1981. It is a good idea to show your own name on stationery.

With partnerships there are many pitfalls. An awfully large number of partnerships collapse. A very firm partnership agreement, drawn up by a solicitor, is a worthwhile precaution. A partner must be someone with whom you can work amicable. In partnerships it is quite useful if one partner is a tip-top sales-person and the other good at figures and finance. Partners must be chosen carefully. To some extent a partnership is a considerable risk, not to be undertaken lightly. Remember failure leads to the assets of both partners being liable to seizure to meet debts. In a limited company with paid up capital this cannot happen. Be careful therefore, in taking a partner, that you think alike in important matters. When you consider how many marriages break up it is not surprising if the same thing happens to partnerships.

A partnership agreement should make it absolutely clear what the relationship is between the partners. If most of the business is going to come through one partner he or she should hold a majority share. Better safe than sorry. The agreement should state who is to do what and for how much. It should be clear what is to happen to profits. I know of part-nerships which failed miserably because one partner wanted to draw out money while the other wanted all money ploughed back into the business for some time. There is nothing to fault a partnership that is well based between people who get on together and there is agreement about the venture.

There are reasons for forming a limited company, the main being that each director's liability is limited. With a new business you may get better credit terms if you do not form a limited company – suppliers will know you have everything at stake. However, if you have everything at stake, you may lose everything.

Running a business in which you stake all you own will make the getting of supplies easier.

In summary:

- If you do not form a limited company and become bankrupt all your possessions can be sold to pay your creditors.

- Choose a partner carefully.

- If you form a partnership do so subject to a proper contract.

12

BUYING AND SELLING A BUSINESS

Let the buyer beware. Remember this maxim in relation to all your purchasing, all your life. Be most particular to keep this in mind when buying a business. Many things appear better than they are. Anyone selling a business to you will present the business in the best light.

There is much to be said for buying a business which is well established. However, remember you could be buying another man's mistakes. Buy with care and only after the fullest consideration and all the professional advice you can get. You may be buying the goodwill of many customers or you may be buying a business on its last legs. Find out which.

Check the history of the business on offer. Has it progressed year by year? Was it beginning to fail because of some local changes? What is the real reason why the owner is selling?

Study what is happening in the district. A new by-pass could kill a business relying on passing trade. One way streets may adversely affect a business ... as can double yellow lines ... and replanning of town centres.

Check what businesses are next to the one you are thinking of buying. Check three each side. Any well-known multiples? If not, are the people there doing well? Check this carefully. Ask, ask, ask.

Are you going to be close to W H Smith, Boots, Woolworth? Are there other buildings for sale nearby? How strong is the goodwill between the present owner and his staff, and between him, his staff, and his customers.

Check with the present owner's creditors. Ask if there has been any recent worsening in the time taken to pay accounts. Check with any customers you can find. Find out if customers like the shop. Talk to the staff. How long have they worked there? What do they think of the trade?

Do not take anything for granted. The seller is entitled to get the best price he can and you are entitled to buy for the lowest price you can.

Get an experienced accountant to check the history of the business, the books, and the stock. If you know the trade, work out for yourself what you think the stock is worth. Pay no more. Remember you are going to have to sell the stock. *You must only pay what the stock is worth to you.* Because an article cost the present owner £1 does not mean it is worth the same to you. The present owner may have been a bad payer or a bad buyer. In either case he will have been paying the wrong price. Find out if the stock has been written down each year. If not, you are perhaps buying at a very bad price. Stock that is not in prime condition is worthless. Pay nothing for old and dirty stock.

Do not believe anything. I have known a man selling a business to put up the prices on all the stock before selling. Take care. Check the purchase prices given to you with the suppliers. Believe nothing you are told, even by the Archangel Gabriel! Investigate everything. If you have no knowledge of prices in the trade, talk to someone who has.

Work out what you can expect to make from the business. Now you know what you can afford to pay for it. Spending a little on proper investigation can save a great deal. Instead of spending twelve months trying to get over a major buying mistake, take two weeks to find out enough to avoid a bad buy.

Whatever you buy look for the profit. No profit, no deal. If you cannot see a worthwhile profit coming in a reasonable time, do not buy. *Do not buy trouble – you can get all you want for nothing.*

Before buying a business consider your competitors.

Sometimes it can pay to buy a business that has been running at a loss. You may be able to buy it cheaply and do better than the present owner. A business can have a potential which has not been realised. The district may be going to improve, and you can take advantage of this. Make sure the trade has a future. Also the area.

Make certain you will have good suppliers.

Do not buy a business which depends for its success entirely on the present owner.

Now let us consider selling a business. It is easier to get a good price for a business if the business has been run with this in mind. Figures will have to be kept to this end.

It will pay to run your business properly and to keep proper books if you intend selling in the future. Failure to keep correct books makes it difficult to prove the real worth of the business. The shopkeeper who is afraid to keep proper books should not be surprised if a buyer does not trust him. Remember that a good buyer will cut down his offer to you if he has any suspicion that your business is not as good as you present it to be.

If you have worked hard for years, you are entitled to a good price for a good business. You must not expect people to pay more than a business can be proved to be worth. Your business should have been run so that it does not entirely revolve around you if you want a good price for the business. If your business will run well without you it will be worth more. A one man business is the worst kind to sell.

Offer your business for sale just ahead of the best period in the year. Be able to show records for the past and to talk of the potential.

A summary of the foregoing reminds you to *let the buyer beware:*

- Buy an established business.

- Study what is happening in the district.

- Examine goodwill with staff, suppliers, customers.

- Check everything.

- Check worth of stock carefully.

- Pay what the stock is worth to you not what someone else paid for it.

- If wishing to sell your business in the future run the business as if you intend to sell – keep proper books.

13

BE A COMPLETE PERSON

There is little profit in business success if it involves loss of health or loved ones. Do not chase business success and forget everything else.

Nothing worthwhile is attained without enthusiasm. It may be necessary to make sacrifices.

Most of the people who say 'Money isn't everything' usually have very little. Money is not everything but it is nice to have just more than enough. Sacrifice and enthusiasm will be needed.

The wise man will want a full life, not a just a business life. He will remember his wife and children. He will remember kindness and patience. He will occasionally bear gifts.

You must have ambition but do not become a slave to ambition.

A person who is complete in all their parts will be better in any one of them.

PART 2

SELLING TO THE RETAIL TRADE

INTRODUCTION

There is a God and a Devil in every one of us. There is latent in us all the power to be what we wish to be. Fighting against this are strong forces of doubt and indecision and sloth.

There is a road we can each travel along if we wish. It is a main road and it is as long as life itself. Branching off this main road are the byways, the blind alleys, and the dead ends. Many of the entrances or approaches to these byways are most alluring and attractive, even enthralling, holding forth much promise of pleasure and ease.

Every man or woman can respond to their own personal God or Devil, and on the decision each makes much depends.

You, the reader, can blaze a trail along the main road, the motorway of a full life, or you can be side-tracked, amused, entertained, and lulled to sleep; left behind by the main stream of life.

It may be pleasant to dally but it is more blessed to arrive. What is your attitude to life? You want to be a salesman? How much else will you sacrifice to be a good salesman? What will you be content with? Do you want a little or a lot? *Your attitude matters* much more than the terms of employment you get or the choice of firm or company to work for. You can work for the best company in the world and still be the worst salesman in the world, or merely mediocre.

You can settle for security in one of those pleasant little byways or you can set your sights high, put your foot down hard on the accelerator, learn all about the steering, be always in the right gear, use to the full the overdrive that saves wear and tear while boosting the output.

If you have read Part 1 of this book, you will have gathered that I am writing about attitudes. Get your outlook right and the job of selling becomes easy and pleasant. Easy because you are doing what comes naturally, and pleasant because you are making friends and money.

You are not entitled to anything, but it is possible to attain whatever you set your heart on. The world owes you nothing, certainly not a living but you can *earn* a living.

The real salesman is the man whose attitude is right, who expects nothing from Grandma State or Social Security, and who does not depend on a minimum salary. Inside this man there burns an unquenchable fire of ambition and he radiates confidence. This man sells.

There is a dearth of good salesmen, of men with the right calibre, whose attitude is right. There is a glut of mediocre and bad salesmen. Ask any sales manager handling a product that is good but needs pushing, and for which a market is not yet fully established.

This dearth of the right men for the job is your opportunity if you can grasp it. The good salesman will never be redundant. A redundant salesman is a contradiction in terms. Either he is not a salesman or he cannot be redundant.

Can you be one of the few? Before answering this question read the pages that follow and examine your attitude. Have the right attitude and the commercial spoils are there for the taking. If your attitude is wrong and you cannot find it in you to change the outlook you have ... if you prefer the easier byways of life and the security so easily found ... then, please do not be a salesman. Be a bus conductor or an office worker or whatever else you find satisfies your desires ... and leave selling to someone else.

14

YOUR ATTITUDE TO
YOURSELF AND YOURS

Why is Winston Churchill regarded as the greatest of all wartime Prime Ministers? Why was he head and shoulders above all other possible candidates for the job at the time? Because of his attitude. He assembled the facts – good and bad – faced them, believed that all obstacles could be overcome, had and inspired confidence, and gave of himself all he had and expected the same from others. A master of salesmen indeed against overwhelming odds. People believed in him despite the very strong possibility that he might be wrong. This is the central art of salesmanship, to inspire confidence regardless of opposition or competition.

Why was it possible for Henry Ford to build an empire? He was a poor man with a good idea. He had nothing that could be called security. He was laughed at. He suffered many privations. However, he knew he was right and his attitude allowed of anything except failure.

Why can one representative go out with a range of samples and only collect a bundle of complaints and a few small orders hardly worth taking, while another with the same range in the same area can smooth out the complaints and collect orders worth ten times as much? Some salesmen are asked to call back later. With them, next month is always going to be terrific until next month comes. Another man gets his turnover every month.

Why do some salesmen think they would always do better if they had the other man's territory? In my considered opinion there is no such thing as a good or bad area – only good or bad salesmen.

Whether or not you will be a good salesman is tied up with your attitude to yourself, your loved ones, the goods you have to sell, the firm you work for and your customers.

This chapter will deal with your attitude to yourself and your family, your pleasures, hobbies, amusements and your time.

The fact that you are reading this book at all may be taken to indicate that you either are or would like to be a salesman. More than that – you would like to be a good salesman. This will be taken for granted from now on. Let me ask you a few questions.

Is it just a job you want? If so, please avoid salesmanship. Is it that you have heard there is big money to be earned, that some firms will supply you with a car and an expense allowance, and you will be able to get away from home and have a good time and a car you could never merit by your own efforts? If so, please do not become a salesman. Forget the whole idea and save a lot of people a lot of trouble.

I do not wish to imply that there is anything wrong with the desire to earn good money or drive a nice car, but there must be something else – a dedication to selling ... an ambition to attain an apparently impossible turnover ... a fire that burns within and spells out in unmistakable terms that to be a salesman is the only worthwhile job in life. This enthusiasm is essential.

Perhaps I can illustrate this point from an experience in my teens, before the Second World War, when selling was much tougher than it is has been in the eighties. My father died when I was quite young and I left school before I needed to in order to earn a living. One of my first jobs, at about sixteen years old, was as a bread roundsman. In those days it meant pulling a very heavy cart in all weathers from 7am to 3pm every day including Saturdays. The baker I worked for had a retail shop in front of the bakery and I noticed that the shop sold biscuits, tea, jam, etc. I asked my employer why he did not give me these things to sell on the round as this would make the round worth more to him and I could perhaps earn myself a commission to augment my rather miserable wage. My employer was not at first pleased with the idea as other bakers did not do this sort of thing, and in any case people could easily come to the shop.

After some further discussion however it was decided that I could try. From then on, instead of just leaving bread on the doorstep, I began ringing the bell and – to the surprise of housewives who were not used much to service of this kind in those days – offered to save them a journey to the shop and informed them that I would always be able to supply their needs at the door. The response was terrific and my income soon became about four times that of many skilled men twice my age.

This is salesmanship. This is the attitude to life that makes a salesman. I had never thought of being a salesman before this. It came naturally. I saw an opening for a service and started to provide it. I was undaunted by the fact that I now worked until 5 or 6pm each day instead of 3pm. I did not expect a rise in basic pay because of the extra hours and would have refused such if it had been offered. I would have said, 'No fear, you increase my commission.' I did not even consider the possibility of failure. This is the attitude that makes a salesman of the kind that is sorely needed today.

I paid a visit to this baker some years later and asked what had happened to the round I had left. This is what happened. The man who took the job next wanted more basic money, refused to try to sell anything, and would work fixed hours only. After about a year the baker gave up the round altogether because he could not find anyone who would take my sort of interest in the job. All the applicants wanted as much as possible for as little as possible. Poor people! I really feel sorry for the man who thinks this is the way to live and bargain with employers. What small minds such people have, what a small world they live in. They would never recognise an opportunity if it stared them in the face all day long. If you are this sort of person throw this book away as it must appear to you to be written in a foreign language.

I would like to continue to illustrate from my own experience. My mother wanted me to get a nice little job in my home town and settle down. I now wanted only one thing – to be a salesman. I had tasted what, to me, was the thrill of making sales and increasing my standard of living by my own efforts. This was the life for me. I could not yet afford a car, but I had a bicycle. I wanted a position selling to the trade and this I got by pretending to be a few years older than I was. I refused to take a salary or expenses despite the fact that I had a very large area to cover. I asked for commission only, making the point that I wanted to be free to earn what I was worth and if I was worth nothing then I was prepared to find this out. I obtained a higher than normal rate of commission for any sales over a certain figure.

This is how I started to cover the greater part of the British Isles for an almost unknown publisher of not very easy-to-sell books. I had made a start. I said to myself, 'I know I can sell, and I will sell.' I knew absolutely nothing about the book trade and had no existing accounts to start with. However, on my bike and later by bus and train and eventually by car, I built up a first rate connection for the lines I was carrying and ultimately was earning more than the managing director of the company employing me!

I could have had security and a settled job in my home town. I might have found myself a nice comfortable cul-de-sac to fossilise in, but I wanted the adventure of travelling and selling. I intended to earn what I was worth, to stand on my own feet. I wanted the satisfaction of a standard of living attained by my efforts.

I was happy and I am still happy when I am selling. I love the work of selling. I have hundreds of friends all over the country, customers whose interests I protect and whose businesses have grown bigger partly because I gave them confidence in the products I myself believed in.

I worked very hard: 9 o'clock found me waiting on the step for the shopkeepers to open up. I worked on in the evening whenever I could persuade people to do business in the evening. I was proud to be the No.1 salesman for my company. I was loyal to my employer. For my money, he was tops and anyone who doubted this had to argue with me about it.

If you would be a good salesman, get the right attitude. Believe in yourself. Study the needs of your customers. Give yourself in your selling. Work out new reasons why your goods should sell or should sell in bigger quantities. Raise the price level at which your customers sell by easy stages. Help them grow. Make your time available to any customer. Turn time into money. Believe you can do this and go and do it.

Laugh at the sceptics, the moaners, the statisticians, the people who know the area and never knew a worse one. Ignore the gloomy prophets, and get on with the job. While the other man is convincing himself his goods will not sell to A and B, get in to see A and B and convince them your goods will sell *anywhere*. Then, you will both be right. Only, you will be richer as well!

This then is the first priority – an attitude of confidence. You must believe in what you sell. If you do not, why should anyone else? Find a territory known as the travellers' graveyard and dig up some customers. Do not disturb the other travellers, however. Leave them alone. Get on with the job you have to do so that when your competitors on the territory wake up it will be later than they think. In fact, too late.

Believe in yourself, radiate confidence, its ever so catching. The average buyer in the retail trade is not all that sure of himself and depends a great deal on the advice given to him. He is frightened and builds a wall of doubt and indifference to hide behind. Your confidence is the trumpet which will bring the walls tumbling down.

If you say, 'I'll never make a good salesman', you are dead right.

The question of an attitude of confidence is well illustrated by the following comparison between the approach of two different salesmen. These two salesmen with similar products called on the same day to offer their goods to Mr Dudley owner of a small store in a Midland market town.

Salesman A said, 'Good morning, Sir, I was out this way so I thought I would call in. Anything you're wanting?'

'Not today', said Mr Dudley glad of such an easy approach to overcome, 'Things are bad, nothing selling.'

Said Salesman A, 'Ah well, I'll call next trip.'

Salesman B arrived soon after and said, 'Good morning, XXX Products, just cannot get around all the calls, worked to death! Never mind! I've got the latest range with me which you'll want to see. Some wonderful lines. You know, the range gets better and better. I'll just get my samples in. Won't be a minute.'

Salesman A looked worried and had cause to be. Salesman B looked confident and had reason to be. Salesman A disliked these small town shopkeepers. Reckoned they had no enterprise, 'dead from the neck up' he thought. Salesman B thought that all small town buyers were a good prospect if only because they did not get so many salesmen calling on them. Also they were more friendly and more in need of help and advice. More loyal to a supplier whose goods sold well. He made them feel important. *He never called because he happened to be nearby. He called because he had something to sell.* He kept records and told the buyer he was selling more than in the year before and that this was the general trend with his products. He never offered to call the next trip. Why should he unless the buyer was away or ill? *He knew the time to sell is now not then.*

One word of warning – the attitude of the top salesman is confident but not superior or condescending. Never dictate, but convince the customer he wants to do what you want him to do. This you will not be able to do unless you are really confident yourself. Learning a lot of sales talk off by heart is a poor substitute for confidence in, and knowledge of, your product. There are teachers of salesmen who suggest this and that method of approach and this and that answer to every situation. This causes me to imagine a pack of parrots going around the country reciting the same line. I do not believe in this nonsense. A salesman is not made by his words and his smart answers. His answers may well be smart but they should be individual and in keeping with his personality. One man can get an order with a phrase which in another man's mouth would sound like a dictation or insult.

Bogus confidence is like a limousine with the smartest lines imaginable and no engine. No personality. Nothing to make it go. You really cannot fool anybody all the time.

There was once a very handsome, apparently convincing sales manager. If he made a call he usually got an order, but he was not liked. When I called on the same customers myself they told me they did not trust him. I always got a better order and a more satisfied customer in the long run. Why? There is always a reason why one man sells more than another and keeps his customers more satisfied. The sales manager mentioned above seemed confident, but it was forced and not part of his personality. He had been taught the need to be confident and therefore acted as if he was. His apparent confidence did not come from within. *It was patter not personal-*

ity. Forced rather than felt. This man caused more doubt in the minds of his customers than confidence.

It is very seldom that I have lost a customer. But representatives I have employed are always losing customers or doing less business with them than before. When this happens I call on the customers myself and find it quite easy to get the kind of order I would expect. Sometimes I have felt that orders from a territory are not good enough and have covered a select number of calls in this area myself and have obtained on average at least four times as much business in one call as my representative produced in a year. I find this easy to do. I expect it to be easy. I believe in myself and my goods and in my ability to outsell any competitor in the country. This is real confidence. It is deep rooted. Not put on. Not learnt from a book or a course on salesmanship. *The real salesman is a personality not a production.* If you lack this inward ability to sell I do not believe any amount of training will make you into a top salesman. It has to be there. An attitude of mind, an outlook. Having that to start with, the salesman can then learn how to make use of his natural talent to the best advantage.

Confidence such as this does not mean bragging nor does it mean false humility. I say, without wishing to brag, that I can sell anything, and sell it better than anybody else. I will increase the turnover on any goods in any area whether I know the trade or not. I know this is so without even a faint doubt. This is the attitude of mind that I think essential in any man who is to reach the top in selling. When an applicant for a sales position says, 'I have a wife and children – will I earn enough?' I say he is not the man I am looking for. He will be so worried lest he does not earn enough that he will have no freedom of mind to take a more positive attitude and improve his standard of living beyond his wildest dreams. Some would-be travellers have only a negative outlook such as 'how much will it cost me to cover the area' rather than the positive approach of 'an area like this should enable me to earn so and so.'

Always the cost rather than the prospect. These people have the wrong attitude and usually do only as well as they expect. It would be foolish to start climbing Mount Everest in the wrong kind of boots; it is just as stupid to launch yourself on a sales career without the confidence which is so essential to success.

Unashamedly and convincingly I tell my customers that the range I offer is the best in the field. They must believe me because I get the business.

Next to confidence in importance as far as the salesman is concerned is his attitude to security. The man who wants to know he is secure whether he sells or not is not the type of man I look for when I need a representative. Neither am I impressed by the salesman wishing to act for me who, when called to an interview, asks first and foremost, 'Will you pay my expenses to the interview?' This reveals an attitude of mind which is not the attitude I wish to observe in a man wishing to sell on my behalf.

I often cover one thousand miles in a week when I go out with goods I have to sell on behalf of a firm for whom I act as agent. My expenses are not paid for me. So what? *I do not count the cost as I am too busy counting the orders.* The man who is always busy counting the cost will never collect big money.

Security often means a fixed salary, expenses paid, and a small commission or bonus. I have never accepted such a position and would not do so. I do not want security. I want opportunity. Given this I will see to it that I am secure. *The greater the security the less the opportunity as a rule. The less the security the greater the opportunity.*

What is your attitude in this respect? Can you stand on your own feet? If you are afraid to work on a results only basis why should you expect to be employed on any other basis? If, for instance, £4000 worth of business would on a commission basis earn you £400 a week, would you rather work for £40 a week guaranteed, £4 a day car allowance, and 2.5% commission? If so, you are either a fool or you are not worth the rate you wish to get. If you can produce £4000 worth of business in a week and earn £400 a week why accept £160? If on the other hand you can only produce £600 worth of business a week how can you expect to be paid £80 for this if your employer must budget for a 10% maximum sales staff cost to allow him to make a legitimate profit? Why should you be paid to be a failure? If you can produce the turnover why work for less than you are worth?

This really brings us back again to the matter of confidence. If you have the confidence to make a star salesman, work on a basis that brings the best reward. It has been said that a man who is willing to work for commission only is either very good or no good. In other words the commission only salesman is either a good salesman who wants to earn in accordance with his ability or else he is a man who would never hold a job on any other basis.

Even looked at from a security-minded point of view, the good salesman is better off on commission only as an agent – because if he is good he will earn well and buy his own security, and, because security earned in this way is one of the most satisfying things in the world and is not limited. A man on a fixed remuneration is secure only in so far as his remuneration allows. He cannot improve his standard of living beyond a certain point. He may have to tailor his living rather drastically to remain secure.

Do not despise the commission-only man. It takes guts to depend on yourself absolutely and it makes for the highest rewards. A man who starts in business with his savings is no different from an agent staking his ability. Both must depend on themselves to show a profit and both are their own master.

A point made in several books on salesmanship is the need for good health, and while it may well be correct to say that an ulcer makes it difficult to enjoy commercial travelling, my own insistence would be firstly on good mental health. In other words the right attitude of mind is the most important asset in a man who would make a success of commercial travelling. Bodily ills can be overcome and often avoided altogether if the mental approach is correct. Many nervous ailments arise as a result of worry. Confidence is the antidote to worry.

Still stressing that the right attitude is of supreme importance may I suggest that this has a further application with regard to the *aim* of the man who would be a successful salesman.

What is your aim? Are your sights set high or low? Many a salesman books small orders because he does not expect to book big ones. When a big order falls into his lap he writes to his firm indicating that this was a red letter day for him. Actually the small orders should be the exception and he should write apologising for them!

Some salesmen earn more than their employers. Others find it difficult to earn enough to dress properly. Nothing succeeds like success. I have on occasions (not as a habit) said to a prospect who is hesitating about placing an order, 'Come outside just a minute. See that Jaguar? That's mine, and please note I work by choice on commission only and have no other income or private means. Does this prove to you that the goods I am offering must sell?' This rather incomplete argument has won me many a customer.

At times a customer or prospect has said that the goods I offer must be dear for me to afford such an expensive car. I answer this by pointing out again that I personally get the whole of my income by way of commission only, and that my personal possessions are a proof of the very wide sale of the products I handle. This clinches orders quite often. This demonstrates that people are impressed by success and want to buy from a successful man.

If you wish to succeed you must appear to have succeeded already.

The salesman is very important to industry. He keeps the factories going. The salesman has every right to feel that he is important to the continued success of commerce. His attitude is that his job matters and the sky's the limit.

You can be a little man or a big man. Your attitude to the future will demonstrate which is the more likely. What do you want? Enough to live a quiet life with a fortnight at Bognor Regis each year? Or do you want to earn the big money that means you can live where you want to live, drive what you want to drive, and take holidays anywhere in the world as you wish.

At examination time some students aim only to pass. Others study hard for honours. Some salesmen aim to sell just enough to get by. The top salesman aims to earn big money. I am most unimpressed by advertisements offering to train salesmen so that they will earn say £15000 a year by the age of thirty five. A salesman who has to wait until he is thirty five to earn £300 a week is not my idea of a top salesman. If he has been working on a fixed remuneration basis he might well be earning £15000 a year at the age of thirty five and very proud of the way he fiddles his expense account to his firm in order

56

to make enough to get by on. On the other hand the man who has had the gumption to work as an agent on commission should have been doing better that this within a few weeks of starting if not immediately.

Another phase of the attitude necessary to the attainment of a successful sales career is a determined conviction that nothing must be allowed to interfere with the job in hand. The would-be salesman who puts his comforts, or his hobbies, or his home, or his wife and children before the job of reaching the top in his sales career will probably never reach the top.

Applicants for positions as salesmen with companies whose sales have been in my hands have often disappointed me because there have been so many things in their minds which took priority over the job of selling. They must be home every night and therefore must finish their last call somewhere between 4 and 6pm. The fact that they may be calling on ladies hairdressers, who are unable to grant interviews of any length until the evening, matters little. It would appear that these gentlemen want more money without any extra effort or inconvenience, certainly without any sacrifice. It must be realised that *the really worthwhile has to be paid for*.

I was talking to a sales manager in an hotel lounge when away on one of my sales sorties. He told me that one of his representatives had failed to send in daily reports for a few days and, in view of this, he had telephoned the salesman's home a 3pm one day to ask the salesman's wife if she would get her husband to ring his office. Imagine his surprise when the salesman answered the call himself. His explanation for being at home in the middle of the afternoon was that he had no more appointments for the day so had returned home early to be with his wife. It had not occurred to him to try to arrange more appointments or to undertake some cold canvas. This man was paid as a full-time representative. Not only does this show the wrong attitude, it is downright dishonest. In fact, I would class such a man as a common crook.

This type of man will never be a top-flight salesman. His attitude to time is all wrong. A salesman must translate as much of his working time as possible into money. In fact the day should be made longer whenever possible by undertaking evening calls. The man who says 'not me' on reading this has absolutely the wrong attitude to succeed in a sales career. Every minute should be regarded as an opportunity to prepare for or to take an order.

The salesman of any experience knows he cannot make up tomorrow for the neglect of today. The call not made is money lost.

The attitude to time is vital. The salesman whose hobbies, home or pleasures eat into his selling time is not the man likely to star in his chosen career. In fact, he is failing to make his job into a career.

The real salesman strives at all costs to make every minute pay. Time for him passes all too quickly. There is never a moment to lose. This does not mean hustle and bustle, just a quiet steady concentration on the target. The super salesman tries to make one more call a day than is regarded as possible, and is often surprised to find that he is late going home or to his hotel. *He is never lost for something to do, and never too busy to do more. He would rather cover another prospect than have a drink with the boys. He only stops selling when there is nobody he can sell to.*

Attitude. It is so important. To the top salesman his job is a joy forever. He never says, 'I don't know why I took this lousy job.' He does not go on strike. He often lacks many other interests at all because he loves his work and would be lost without it. He would much rather work than play.

This attitude which is so essential to the man who would reach the top in the field of selling has other virtues also. A man who is happy in his work makes a better husband than one who is not happy in his daily routine. He is mentally healthy. He is wide awake. Alertness is his middle name. He usually puts the same enthusiasm into all he does as this has become second nature to him. This enthusiasm is infectious and helps to make friends and influence people more than anything else he might do to this end.

The sacrifices made in order to become a successful salesman bring the highest reward any man can ask. A healthy mind, an active body, a full stomach.

15

YOUR ATTITUDE TO
THE GOODS YOU SELL

There was a popular song that assured us what is said in the Bible 'ain't necessarily so' and be that as it may, one thing that is said in that book should be remembered daily by every salesman. Namely, that faith can move mountains.

Honesty is the best policy in salesmanship. Faith is one of the first essentials. An honest man with faith in his goods is irresistible.

If your attitude is not one of faith and honest belief in the goods you have to offer it would be better that you choose a different occupation. A salesman who does not believe in the goods he offers for sale is unable to be convincing. He cannot expect to be. A salesman without faith is like a watch without the works. The outward appearance is apparently in order but there is nothing to make the man 'tick'. An honest mans' belief in his goods is what some people mean by personality, or at least, it is a facet of such personality. If it is lacking no amount of veneer or sales training will take its place.

From the foregoing it will be clear that it is of the greatest importance that the salesman should choose his employer carefully. It is not necessary that the firm he works for should be a household name but he must choose a firm with honest trading methods and one offering reasonable value for money. Having done this, his honest faith in the goods he offers will bring in the business.

The man who says, 'Got to do something old man,' or 'I don't think much of the lines, but it's a living,' will never be worth a row of beans as a salesman.

Be proud. *Pride comes before a sale.* I am in the fortunate or unfortunate position of not only selling large quantities of goods, but of buying these goods in the first place. I therefore have the opportunity of observing salesmen from some very large companies and some quite small firms. I find myself responding to the man who obviously is proud of his goods, who expects to get an order because he is utterly convinced that goods better than this are unobtainable. On the other hand I buy hesitantly from the man who says, 'I thought there might be something in the range that would interest you.' Something else I notice – the first man mentioned above stays with his firm a long time, the second man often does not appear again, or if he does it is with another house.

If you cannot believe in the goods you sell, either change your employer or change your occupation.

This pride, this belief in the goods offered is not blind faith. It is reasoned and logical. It has a basis in fact. The clever salesman is the one who can think of the most convincing way of presenting his goods so that his prospects will believe as he does.

The need to present one's goods convincingly necessitates knowledge of, as well as belief in, the goods concerned. It is most important that a salesman should learn about the lines he offers to other people so that he can answer criticism, explain prices, and justify the product in every way.

A good salesman knows why one item is dearer than another. Perhaps I may illustrate this from the costume jewellery trade in which I am at present engaged on the sales promotion side. Two necklaces which look almost alike at first glance can cost quite a different price for several reasons. One may be threaded on cotton and the other on nylon; one may be made up of plastic beads and the other of glass beads; the difference in the cost of a clasp may be 10 pence or so; the way in which the ends of the rows are secured can have quite a bearing on the final price; the dearer necklace may be composed of beads sold exclusively to one supplier or used exclusively in one style of necklace. All these things make a difference to price, and a salesman who cannot give the reasons for such differences is beaten before he starts. The same thing applies with brooches which may have stones either stuck in or claw-set. One can be twice the price of the other. There is also the matter of the pin at the back, which could be rivetted or just clamped. An item in jewellery can be untarnishable or otherwise, nickel-plated, silver-plated, or sterling silver, anodised, gold-plated, rolled gold, or gold. Many items in the range may look alike but the work undertaken in their making can be very different, as may also be the expected life of the article.

In the book trade a novel may be cloth bound or Linson bound. Pages may be sewn or glued together, and so on. The way a thing is made, and the length of life that can be expected from it, contribute to its price. When the customer asks, 'What's the difference?' the good salesman knows, and believes in the reason he gives, and is able to justify his price confidently.

In all trades there are reasons for prices. Reasons for packs. Reasons for delivery times. Reasons for trading terms. The salesman who would scale the heights in his profession knows and can justify the reasons.

The salesman with a good commodity to sell need never be afraid, always providing he believes in the commodity, and has at his fingertips the reasons for price, pack, delivery times, terms, etc.

The salesman who is frightened of prices might as well be dead. The salesman with nothing to sell but price has nothing to sell. There will always be someone willing to do a thing cheaper, but will it be as well done, as well packed, as widely advertised, etc. Know the reasons for the prices of your goods and be fearless in their presentation. After all, the salesman is engaged and paid to sell his firm's products at their prices and on their conditions. This is his job. There would be no need for salesmen if everything could be made available for less than it is worth. The salesman must believe in his goods and understand the reason for his prices. He should tell his customers that they can always buy cheaper somewhere else but not the same goods, or if the same goods, then not with the same service in the way of advertising, supplies, sales aids, etc. There is never the slightest reason to be afraid of a fair price. *The competitor who is always cutting prices will probably cut his throat in the end and you can go to the funeral.* Over and over again I have known competitors, who were undercutting prices at which I had to sell, sink into oblivion after a few months or a year or two.

My belief in the goods that I sell is such that I do actually tell my customers to buy elsewhere if they want to buy at the lowest possible price in every case. I tell them that I am not concerned only with price. I am concerned with offering fair value for money, something a little different or exclusive, backed up by a good repair service and, in some cases, national advertising. I am not the least concerned that they are able to buy for £3.80 a line I offer for £4. The interesting point is that the sales of the company I am associated with continue to rise year after year. The business we do with individual customers is always on the increase. The lines we sell to the retailer move off the shelves much quicker than those of our competitors. Price is not the first consideration at any time, but quality, service, and advertising count for just as much or more. It is in the retail trader's interest to deal with dependable and conscientious people who intend to build a worthwhile business and who, in doing so, must help to build the businesses of their customers.

It must be most exasperating to the salesman selling on the cheap to find that quite a few retailers are not tempted by his price inducements. This is doubtless because these customers have found suppliers on whom they rely for goods with a difference and dependable service. These qualities are worth more to the retailer than the odd pence he can save dealing with the price-cutting wholesaler. A fair price is a good price.

Good salesmen make little businesses big because they believe in the products they offer and know how to present such products in the best possible light. The poor salesman is the one who cannot sell unless he is the cheapest in the field. He has no idea of how to sell on any other basis. If he meets a retailer who tells him that an item can be obtained 10% cheaper he writes to his sales manager about this and asks how he is expected to sell if his firm is dearer than other people. I feel very sorry for any man who writes such letters, and even sorrier for the firm unfortunate enough to be employing him, unless of course the goods are not value for money.

A point worth mentioning is that of the salesman's attitude to competitors. When confronted with the fact that a customer has bought from a competitor what should the salesman say?

He most certainly should not abuse his competitor. This is a matter of attitude again. A man who believes in his goods, understands his prices and appreciates the reasons for his firms' trading terms, is never negative, always positive. Abuse of a competitor is only negative. It is an endeavour to persuade a customer not to buy something from somebody. A positive attitude is more likely to be successful – namely an attempt to persuade a customer to buy something from you.

In the face of competition talk only of the reasons why a customer should buy from you. Never waste time talking about why he should not buy from somebody else. The customer does not like this, in any case. He may feel that you are on the defensive because you know you are being beaten. I never mind hearing that a competitor has been abusing me. It cheers me up considerably because to me it shows that I have been hurting my competitor and that he has no positive way of overcoming my products. If a customer tells me he has made a good buy from a competitor of mine, I say, 'Good, now you have the opportunity of making an even better buy from my range, which as you know is the most varied in the trade, the best selling in the country and the most advertised.' I go on to say that not only do we sell to our customers but we sell for them as well by advertising and by point-of-sale aids. I talk about the increase in our turnover, the number of exclusive lines we have to offer, etc, etc. I do not say one word against the competitor except, if it is a matter of cheapness, I sometimes say that no doubt the competitor in question knows what his goods are worth, just as I know what my goods are worth.

To some extent the good salesman is an educationalist. He studies his products so that he can educate to the latest, the best. This is part of the salesman's job, to educate the retailer, especially the very busy one-man shop retailer who does not have time to study trade papers. This man may be suspicious of any line he is not already familiar with, and it is here that a good representative is worth his weight in gold, in that he is able to provide facts about the new product instead of going away satisfied with the statement, 'I promise I'll order it if I'm asked for it.' He should be told there is little likelihood of his being asked for it as his prospective customers will have already bought it somewhere else. He should be educated to lead and not to follow fashion. Here, again, the man who believes in his lines and understands them will take the business.

The salesman must persist in the statement that his goods are the best available. A good salesman is not easily shaken from the standpoint thus maintained. I have never been shaken from this assertion, mainly because I understand my lines, and the points for and against, far better than most of my customers. It is most important that every salesman should feel himself to be in this position. It is useless being the second-best, or fairly good, or worth a trial. The goods offered must be presented as the best available. The position to reach is that where the retailer fears a loss of trade if he should not have your lines. He will not feel this unless your attitude to your goods is the correct one of faith and knowledge.

If for some reason I am a little late making an expected call on a customer, perhaps two weeks late because of an excess of calls to be covered, I like that customer to write in saying he is worried as he does wish to have further supplies and does not wish to buy elsewhere. Failing this, I like the greeting, 'Oh! I am glad you've come. We were getting a little worried, and we prefer to deal with you. One or two others have been around but we did not buy from them.' The right attitude to the goods you sell will get you this kind of customer who will be loyal to you and your products, and the salesman (so-called) who calls on such customers and criticises your products will be sent away with a flea in his ear.

The attitude to one's goods, if correct, will mean that however large the range to be carried, all goods will be shown. The good salesman has no preconceived ideas as to some samples selling and others not. Neither is he too idle to carry all the samples when he goes selling. Sometimes when I have gone out into an area from which the expected amount of business has not been forthcoming I find that the man on the territory has not been showing the full range and the customer often has had no idea of the wide range of goods we offer, and this is why the orders have been smaller than I expected.

A salesman working for me sometimes remarks that it is a pity such and such a line has been withdrawn. Like the woman who says she has simply nothing to wear, this salesman feels that the withdrawal of that line means he has nothing to sell. This is the wrong attitude. It is not possible, for many reasons, to keep every line in a range going for ever, and to become too dependent for your income on one or two lines is wrong. If a good seller is withdrawn from a range this merely provides an opportunity to turn another line from a fair seller to a good seller in its place.

The top salesman always is on the lookout for new reasons why his goods should sell. For instance, to take another example from the costume jewellery trade, gilt chain necklets were selling very well for some time, then the demand cooled off. Somebody thought of a new market for these chains and they began to appear as a replacement for the usual strap or handle on handbags. This is an excellent illustration of how to adapt a line to a new outlet thus prolonging its sale.

Brooches always sell but at times they sell less. An ingenious salesman immediately began to sell more brooches by suggesting that some would be very nice as hat brooches and others as belt brooches. Just a matter of suggesting a different position to wear the article increased its sale. Make this your attitude to your goods, one of alert watchfulness for any market that suggests itself to you.

- Have faith.

- Increase knowledge.

- Seek new outlets.

- Believe.

- Know.

- Sell.

16

YOUR ATTITUDE TO
YOUR EMPLOYER

The cause of much loss of time and money in industry today is the result of bad employer–employee relationships. As a rule such relationships where salesmen are concerned do not come in for very much discussion. This is a pity. The salesman's attitude to his employer is of the greatest importance. The salesman knows his employer better than the customer to whom he may be no more than a name and not always that. If the customer can see that the salesman does not think very highly of his employer it is unlikely that this will lead to much confidence on the part of the customer as far as his dealings with the firm are concerned, and this may mean smaller orders.

When you go out on the road with a range of samples, you go on trust. Your employer has to trust you or have a detective following you all day, and this not practical. Therefore, the position of a traveller is one of trust. The top salesman can be trusted. He wants to succeed and his success is to the benefit of his employer. If you cannot be trusted you cannot reach the top as a salesman. The top flight salesman is trustworthy. His employer never has to worry as to whether the job is being done or not. The orders that come in prove that it is being done, and *the goodwill that a good salesman creates is one of the major assets of any business.*

The successful salesman is proud to work for his firm or company. He will, by every word, build up the confidence of customers in the firm that provides him with his livelihood. He does this without any direct intention because his attitude toward his employer is correct. The salesman who never has a good word to say for his firm has little to recommend him or his products. In hotel lounges in the evenings I have heard salesmen talking about their employers as though they are only waiting for the opportunity to leave their employment. It is a pity they do not do so at once. I could not work for a firm I do not respect.

The firm I work for is my commercial God as far as my customers are concerned. I may well have differences of opinion with the firm, but this is never allowed to creep into my conversation with anybody outside the firm. This is commercial integrity and without such loyalty a salesman is unlikely to climb very far up the ladder of success. Think about this. If you were a buyer, who would you prefer to buy from? A firm represented by men who obviously are proud to be employed by their firm or from another company whose salesmen never seem to be very enamoured of their employer? There is only one answer to this question.

There is no need to be shy of the fact that you are delighted to be working for your company. Remember that a shrewd buyer feels that a firm with happy and contented employees is probably a firm whose dealings are in all respects fair and above board. Some travellers give the impression that their employers are a bunch of crooks always trying to do them out of their commission. Either this is not true or, if it is, why on earth do the travellers continue in their employment?

The attitude that makes for success is that of the salesman who is never satisfied with the results he produces. He knows the range is good. He feels privileged to be carrying such a range and he cannot produce enough turnover. He plots and plans as to how to increase month by month and year by year the turnover in his territory. He regards it as an honour to attain the best figures among all the salesmen working for his firm. He identifies with the firm. Their interests are his interests. He says 'We' not 'I'. He becomes part of the company he works for. His loyalty is absolute. These are the hallmarks of the man who succeeds because he deserves to. The man who is supposed to be working full time for one company but who carries sidelines from other concerns is a crook, a dishonest and disreputable liar. If I was a buyer in a retail shop I would have nothing to do with such salesmen. A liar in one respect may be a liar in all respects. A man who is dishonest toward his employer is likely to be dishonest to his customers also. The man to employ as a salesman or to buy from is the man who honestly and diligently represents his employer.

Integrity means that a salesman gives his all to the promotion of his company's goods. It means that he does not cook his expense account. It means that he does as he would be done by.

Crooks always seem to prosper but it is the man of integrity who really prospers. The top salesmen are gentlemen in every sense of the word. They are conscientious and diligent. Sincerity is their hallmark. You cannot be a clever dick and reach the top in selling. One proof of this is seen in the fact that the honest firms always surpass the efforts of the crafty, crooked and catch-penny concerns who endeavour to compete with them. The same is true of salesmen.

To do well is the only praise a real salesman needs. His orders are his Oscar. His turnover is his testimonial. He does not feel affronted if his sales manager does not praise him for every order he takes. It is his job to take orders.

It is part of a salesman's duty to protect his employer's interests. For this reason he will consider the credit-worthiness of the customers he calls on and will not book big orders from bad payers just to collect the commission regardless of whether his firm receives payment or not. The top salesman does not tell the customer that it does not matter if they keep to the firm's trading terms or not. He does not say that goods unsold will be exchanged in order to book business. *The only order worth taking is the order that is going to be paid for.* Anybody can sell goods to a man who has no intention of paying for them. The salesman of any worth will not do this, and will indicate to his employer what he thinks of any account he calls on. He will not expect to earn money on a bad risk. After all, if his employer has too many bad debts he may be forced out of business, in which case the salesman is out of a job, and perhaps a lot of other people are also made redundant. This brings us back to honesty and integrity. Any other attitude towards one's employer is a wrong attitude and will mitigate against outstanding success in the field of selling.

The good salesman will be glad to submit reports to his employer. After all, such reports help to build up a mailing list and lead to business at a later date even if not immediately. It is not a nuisance to make reports. It is a duty to the man who pays your salary and/or commission.

The top salesman will do what the average salesman does not do. He will work when they are at the pub in the evening. He will always put his job first. The top flight man is usually exhausted after a good days' work because he gives his all and has little or nothing left. The first class entertainer gives his all. This is what makes him first class. The same is true of the top salesmen. They give all they have to do their job – the job of selling. They project their personality fully into their jobs. They do not do what they have to do and no more. To do less than everything possible to produce turnover is foreign to their nature. If you cannot find it in yourself to adopt this attitude to your job and your employer please do not clutter up the roads, but leave the job of selling to those who can.

- The top salesman must be completely trustworthy.

- He must have pride in his firm.

- His loyalty is absolute.

- He is never satisfied with his turnover.

- He respects his employer's credit terms.

- He regards it as his duty to submit reports.

- He will always put his job first.

17

YOUR ATTITUDE TO
YOUR CUSTOMERS AND PROSPECTS

Other things being equal, *a buyer will buy the most from the salesman he likes the most.* For this reason the salesman's attitude to his customers is of the greatest possible importance. I am most grateful for the fact that I can honestly say that I have hundreds of friends all over the country whose orders I can count on without any doubt at all, and in the face of any and all competition. When short of finance, at one time, to continue building a business which on the sales side I had expanded a little too quickly and slightly overreached myself, I had to cease buying for a while and was unable to supply all the orders I could easily get. Several hundred of my customers filled up with small quantities from other sources in the meantime but once I had arranged the necessary finance to continue stocking as before they expressed their pleasure at this and immediately ceased buying elsewhere and gave me their business again. These people are my friends and their loyalty to me has often delighted me. *You cannot demand loyalty, and if it is not forthcoming you do not deserve it.*

The attitude of the top salesman is always one of friendliness. This does not mean talking about the customer's hobbies or family but just the showing of a sincere interest in the customer and the success of his business. The taking of the customer's point of view in so far as you sell to him with his best interests in mind. The customer should feel that he is being helped rather than talked into something. Say 'You' more than 'I'.

After all, it is a very satisfactory experience to see a

customer's sale of your goods constantly increasing because you have advised him well. A lady who had started a business a few months earlier said to me, 'I've had some wonderful help from you and from some suppliers of other lines that I stock, and you will all get my continued business. The people who stocked me up with the rubbish and advised me badly will get nothing.' She went on to complain of the condescending attitude of some travellers and the couldn't-care-less attitude of others. She was a friendly soul but a little nervous and not very knowledgeable. A perfect prey for the unscrupulous salesman, but at the same time the type of person who would be loyal for ever to anyone who advised her well and studied her interests. It pays to make friends in business. Not only do you keep their business but they will find new customers for you. *A new friend made in business is the beginning of a chain*, the first link only. Tracing back through my lists of accounts I can, in one case, trace fourteen customers who were recommended from the one original account. There have been cases where a retailer from one part of the country on holiday in another county has been given our name and address by one of our customers after admiring the range on show in our customer's shop. It is then that I learn how strongly our customers favour us. They say, 'You couldn't deal with nicer people, and the range is marvellous.'

If you cannot make friends you cannot make sales. Those who dislike people cannot sell. Dislike breeds dislike. A smile brings an answering smile. Sincerity finds responsiveness.

Friendliness leads to confidence and confidence means good orders. A condescending attitude makes the customer feel small and order small if at all. Friendly aggressiveness nets the business but a bullying, I-know-better-than-you, aggressiveness only builds resistance. Some salesmen read that they must be forceful and aggressive and wonder why they do not get the business. Nobody could be more forceful and aggressive than they are but they forget that, just as justice needs to be tempered with mercy, so does aggressiveness and forceful selling need an underlining friendliness.

Ask yourself, how many friends do I have among my calls? How many people am I delighted to see? How many of my customers are obviously pleased to see me? How many greet me with a smile and a quip? How often do you feel at home with your customers and they with you? How often is doing business a pleasure? How often can you feel that the customer likes to do business with you? Or, alternatively, does it happen that the customer is always busy when you call. Has he said to an assistant as you approach, 'I can't stand that man, tell him I'm out.' This is the test of friendliness. If a customer of mine has had a bad time and cannot buy when I call he apologises profusely. Shows me the position honestly. Assures me he has not bought elsewhere and is genuinely sorry not to be able to place an order. He usually wants to talk and ask advice and to know how things are doing elsewhere, and listens intelligently to any suggestions I am able to make to improve sales. These people are my friends. I know I will get any business that is going.

One word of warning that is not meant to be given in a cynical manner. It must be remembered that even when the friendliness is absolutely genuine it must be a means to an end. *The salesman's job is not just to make friends but to sell to the friends he makes.* When checking once on poor sales in an area customers said over and over again what a nice man our Mr X is, but they did not give him the orders. In this case he was a nice inoffensive little person but he had no sales drive. That is why I have said above, 'Other things being equal a buyer will buy from the salesman he likes most.' You must not only make friends but also influence people. The confidence, the drive, the aggression must be there – but underlined with a current of friendliness that is felt but does not detract from the main purpose.

The friendly but confident and forceful salesman makes the customer feel important. Never make your prospect feel small. Compliment him on his window display, his modern well-lit shop, his good taste. Tell him he can sell your goods. Tell him that customers with half his drive are doing quite well with the lines you offer. Create in him the confidence you feel yourself. Remember friendliness creates confidence. A superior attitude will only alienate the customer. Do not be too big for your shoes or you may be told you are too big for his purpose.

The great thing about the friendly approach which does not lack the necessary drive is this – *goodwill cannot easily be destroyed*. You can prove this easily. Try to take the business away from a firm whose salesman has created goodwill with his customer. You will not find it easy. The creation of goodwill is your insurance policy against bad times. When business is slack you will still get some business. The objectionable traveller will be refused in the same circumstances however big and important his company is and he thinks he is.

Friendliness is based on truth. Keep your statements believable. In social life a friendship is often broken by a lie. A lie can lose you a customer. If you promise sole rights in an area stick to this agreement. If a line does not sell well, say so. I sell a lot of bad sellers by being honest about them. I tell the customer the line has not sold well but perhaps he can see an outlet for it that other retailers have not seen. I never say it is a wonderful seller unless it is and I can prove it.

Remember that *all great businesses are built on integrity*. Let the smart alecs do as they wish. You will outstay them all. Never get known for sharp dealing. A customer will forgive a bad delivery service if you explain the difficulties that caused it, but how do you explain a lie?

Another point about friendliness that is worth a mention is that a friendly atmosphere is restful, and it pays to make it restful for a customer to order. If the customer is convinced of your friendship and integrity he will relax in your presence and will lose his suspicions. He will be guided by you as to the best lines to buy. He will come to believe in your good judgement. He will trust you. Once you have this trust never betray it. You are not meant to be a confidence trickster. You are a salesman. You want to call again and sell again and again to the same person.

If you feel in your personal life that everything has gone wrong and you lack courage to face the future, and your self confidence is reduced to nil, to whom do you then turn? Not to the very superior man next door who never seems to have any trouble except the smell under his nose. No, you turn to a friend. A friend is the person who can restore your self confidence because you believe in him and you feel that he will not mislead you. You feel that he will genuinely put your interests first and will like to help you. The good salesman is able, because of his friendly and sincere attitude, to bolster the customer's confidence. The smart alec only makes the customer feel more insecure. The superior person likewise because he cannot come down to the right level to be of any use. This is why the complete salesman is able to revive trade that has slipped. He can build confidence in other people.

When asked why she likes a certain friend a girl might say, 'We speak the same language.' To speak the same language as a customer is most important. Do not talk over the head of the person you are selling to. Friends do not do this. That is why some people do not make friends because they cannot speak the same language as those with whom they would be friends. You cannot be superior and friendly.

Customers do not like being given lectures on how to run their businesses. Friendly advice they will listen to. Even criticism if sincerely given will not go amiss. The average person wants to learn but not from the smug and complacent.

Always act as though pleased to see your customer, just as two old friends who have not met for some time. I always remember one man who used to sell to me. His whole person radiated pleasure whenever he called to see me. I felt liked and this is a nice feeling which leads to an unbending of the professional buying attitude.

Act as if you are selling to your best friend. It makes a difference to the customer you treat in this way. He will respond to this kind of approach, perhaps slowly at first, but friendship is like the measels, it spreads.

Nurse your good prospects into friends who will really support you in bad times and good. A customer is just a call to some salesmen, to others a call on a customer is a pleasure for both.

You do not forget a good friend. Never forget a customer and don't let a customer forget you. *Be the person your customer thinks of immediately your kind of products are mentioned,* so that if competitors call the customer will hesitate to place a very large order with them because you will be calling again.

The foregoing paragraphs have stressed the need for a friendly attitude toward customers providing that the main purpose of your calls is not overlooked – namely to sell. This need for friendliness however must not be taken to mean that the representative must knuckle under to any kind of treatment from customers and prospects. Good friendship means equality. You should not act superior to your customer, but neither should the customer expect to treat you as an underling, or be rude to you. There is no reason why you should put up with unnecessary rudeness or a condescending attitude on the part of buyers. The best buyers never treat salesmen in this way, but there are some little tin gods who think that they can make a salesman feel small, and that he will put up with this to get an order. I am totally against this and have never permitted any customer to treat me in this manner. *I believe in selling from strength and not from weakness.* I do not beg for orders. No really good salesman ever does so. Let me illustrate this by reminding you of the incident related in the first part of this book.

In my early days of selling when salesmen were a little more trodden on than they are today, I was pioneering for a not very well known firm.

A retailer I called on asked, 'Who do you represent?'

'So and So,' I said.

'Never heard of them,' he said in a bullying tone.

'Well,' said I, 'I never heard of you until today.'

This was my way of showing that I was not prepared to be trodden on by anybody. We discussed the fact that there was no need for a buyer to be rude or superior in order to guard from buying the wrong goods. We also discussed the fact that he could not know everything or everybody, and that occasionally somebody might just do something good without him knowing about it, and that it was a buyer's job to look at everything and buy the best. I got my order.

When I was selling to retailers for the first time at the age of about seventeen, I called on a store and seeing that the buyer I wanted to interview was busy I waited over by another department. After a while a hand struck me, not lightly, on the shoulder and an aggressive voice said,

'Who are you?'

I turned and said, 'And who the hell are you?'

Again I got my order. If I had been very meek and mild I would not have done. *It is no good trying to make a career of selling if you are afraid to say boo to a goose.*

The good salesman probably earns ten times as much

money as the average buyer and has no need to suffer any kind of treatment which is not polite and correct. He should of course be polite and correct in return.

The only way to do business is as equals who wish to help each other. The buyer would not be very happy if all salesmen stopped calling on him. The habitually rude and overbearing buyer needs bringing down a peg or two. Some buyers think their time is valuable and a salesman's time is of no consequence. I always correct this assumption when I meet it. A buyer once made an appointment with me and then decided not to keep it because she felt like doing something else.

'You have to put up with this in your job,' she said.

'Not on your life,' said I. 'If you do not intend to keep your appointment with me, despite the fact there is no reason why you should not do so, then you can get your supplies from someone who does not mind being treated in this way because he is so desperate for orders. I came forty miles to see you today and under no circumstances will I come again if you do not see me now.'

I got my order this time also, but if I had not I would not have minded. As I explained to the buyer concerned, my goods sell, and if she had treated me in the way that she had apparently intended, I would have sought to put my goods in a rival establishment, and I would have worked hard to do so.

There was another occasion when a representative of mine had an appointment with a store buyer. He drove sixty five miles from his home to keep this appointment. He announced his arrival to an assistant who alerted the buyer, at the time engaged in making notes in a book. The buyer continued his note making for some time and then walked out of the store. My representative asked the assistant where he had gone, and was told she did not know, but she confirmed that the buyer was aware the salesman had arrived for the appointment. This was reported to me. I wrote to the store directors about the incident, telling them I was pleased we did business with them, but I had no intention that my representative should be treated in this manner and perhaps they would like to come to us if they wanted goods as I could see no future in sending salesmen to call on people who acted so ignorantly and discourteously. I received an apology from the directors who did call on us and placed a bigger order than we had ever had before from this store.

A salesman should be courteous, sincere and friendly, but there is no reason at all why he should put up with calculated rudeness. A top salesman earns at least £15000 a year. Why should he put up with the overbearing attitude of some little men who could never do his job, and who obviously cannot do their own.

For this reason I say that equality is the attitude. Neither the buyer nor the salesman is the boss. The one needs the other. Also, it is important that the salesman is able to sell from strength. He must be confident. Such a man will not easily bow the knee to anyone.

Some customers have told me at times they prefer to see me rather than a representative I send because I am more cheerful and friendly. They say too many salesmen talk too much about anything but business. I get on with the job while retaining a cheerful and friendly atmosphere without wasting their time with funny stories and talk about my family or politics or the next world war! I never waste a customers' time. There is fun in business, fun in selling. My customers and I laugh an awful lot during a selling session. Yet, we are all the time attending to business. I say, *cut the cackle and get on with the job.* Project a cheerful personality and the whole time spent on your visit will be interesting, amusing, and worthwhile.

So far, in thinking of the salesman's attitude to customers we have discussed friendliness and equality. Of equal importance is perseverance. Henry Ford, a hero of mine, said, 'It is always too soon to quit.' Especially in cold canvas work is perseverance essential. Make as many calls as you can and the law of averages will work for you. Call enough and you will sell enough providing of course that you have the right attitude to your work, your goods, your employer, your customers.

Even when calling for the first time on prospects who do not know me or the goods I offer, it is seldom that I fail to get an order. I make a friendly but confident approach, and then I stick like a leech. I act to some extent independently as though I had enough customers already, but seeing such a nice shop etc, etc. It works like a charm. I act as though I expect

.. order, not casually. *I do not take kindly to the suggestion of calling next time.* Now is the time to do business.

I am extremely in earnest always. It is a matter of considerable bewilderment to me to find such a wonderful shop without our goods. To be earnest is to convince. *The casual salesman has a casual income. The real salesman has a real income.*

Some days do not start well. Persevere. Keep at it. Get that first order, then get another. The best time to get an order, someone remarked, is when you've just got one. No salesman worthy of the name, who keeps calling can possibly fail to get business. The good salesman is not easily put off. In fact, buyers usually recognise a successful man and will talk to him.

Having mentioned the necessity of friendly sincerity, of holding your own as an equal and selling from strength, and the need for perseverance, the rest of this chapter will throw out various pointers and hints which help towards success in dealing with customers of all kinds.

One aim of the salesman who is going to reach the top in his trade is to increase the quantity of goods he sells without a relative increase in time spent doing so. To achieve this a friendly relationship with the customer is the basis. He will then be helpful. You can explain that you have more customers than you know what to do with and that you wish to give the best service possible to all of them. This, you point out, will be impossible if you have to call twice anywhere for an order. Ask their help and, if you have gained their confidence and their friendship, customers will wish to help you. Point out that you can always arrange to invoice goods at the date wanted but could they be kind enough to order when you call, and have the goods when they want to. This will enable you to make more successful calls. It will also avoid the possibility of someone else getting the order between your calls. If you cannot arrange this you have failed to build up the relationship with your customers that is essential to the greatest success in the job of selling. You should be able to book orders in January for Easter. Why not? I always do. I believe that every month I should attain good figures. There are no bad months, only bad customer relationships. The second rate salesman is always calling back, always believing in next month. The top salesman is always taking orders.

Every salesman should remember that time spent in his car is time when he is not earning. He should work out a system of calls that allows him as much time as possible in front of his customers. Again it will help if his customers in any one area will see him on the same day or at least during the same week.

May I be permitted to repeat again that the art of salesmanship is to make the customer want the goods you have to sell. In other words the salesman must create desire. To do this his attitude to the customer must be correct. His sincerity and honesty must be apparent. His confidence must shine like a beacon.

The salesman must make use of the profit motive. He must show the prospect how much profit he will make. *The buyer's attention must, to a certain extent, be directed away from how much he is spending and focussed on how much he will make.* Be positive in your selling. Don't talk about how much it will cost a prospect to stock your goods. Tell him how much he will make a month if he does stock your goods. Tell him he cannot afford not to stock them. Be definite in your presentation of the facts regarding both the goods and the profit that can be expected. Never be indecisive. The definite man gets the firm order. The man who is not so sure of his facts can never be sure of anything.

Taking it for granted that you have a good range to sell, let the products prove themselves. If you have a large range of goods to show there is no point in trying to ram any one of these lines down the throat of a buyer who does not like the particular line. I have had a salesman who did this until the customers asked me to see to it that this particular salesman did not call on them again. With a wide range of goods, and provided you have established a friendly relationship with your customers, you will get an order to the value you desire without needing to appear to be telling the customer his business. There is a time to push a line and a time not to do so. The way to sell to one person may not be the way to sell to another. There are people with different levels of intelligence and they should be talked to in different ways. The good salesman is adaptable and knows instinctively the way to deal with different people. One of the marks of a good salesman is that he knows when to press and when not to press. He knows when he is talking to a buyer who knows his business. He can distinguish between the professional buyer and the beginner in business who needs advice and a bit of a push. To try to sell an unwanted line to a very intelligent buyer who does not want it is sheer lunacy! Remember a buyers' time is important and you should not waste it talking about the lines he does not want to buy. By all means try to sell each line but do not keep on trying once you can see the buyer knows his business and will not want the particular line you are showing. Get the unwanted lines out of the way quickly so that time is not wasted.

You might be surprised to know how many complaints I receive that representatives take too long showing the range, that they talk too much about everything, and keep trying to push teenage lines in shops catering for the middle-aged and vice versa. That an order which could easily be taken in an hour is stretched to two hours or more. That in the end they tell the representative they do not need supplies or goods are not selling, and they buy from another company whose representative is able to take an order in the minimum of time.

You may easily lose business by being too long winded. Also the quicker you get the order the more orders you can take in a day.

Another pointer to sales success is planning. Your sales effort should be planned and not hit or miss. Consider the best time to get an order, the best time of year, the best day of the week, the best time of the day. Plan to arrange that your calls follow one another in a natural sequence. Try not to go to A then Z, and back to K. Make your economy one of time and not only monetary cost.

On every call assume that you are going to get an order. Act as if you expect this. Once you start showing a few lines have your order book ready. Make it appear to the customer that it is natural for you to get orders whenever you call. Begin by writing the order as soon as possible. If the customer comments on this say that no doubt he is a busy man and you thought he would appreciate that you had no intention of wasting his time.

It often is useful with a new customer or a prospect who is a little frightened of ordering, to show one or two orders booked from other people. Do not be afraid to do this. Talk about your customers and things they do to promote sales such as running Christmas Clubs, selling to whist drive organisers, ladies nights among the masons or whatever. Tell them of methods of display that other customers have found effective.

Above all, do not ever be frightened of price. *Make the usefulness of an article more important than the price.* Point out that more profit with less work is possible if the customer sells more expensive lines. Make an issue of the exclusiveness of any of your lines; say you can build a reputation for having goods that are a little different. Point out that nobody can buy a Rolls Royce for the price of a Ford Sierra. State that those people who buy exclusive goods will expect to pay more. In other words, stress the benefits and the cost will look after itself. Tell the customer he can be proud to sell such nice lines. Above all, where price is concerned have one price for all customers, and sell to accredited dealers only. Do not sell your lines to private persons to resell in factories or to their friends.

If you cannot resist cooking your expense account if you have one, at least do not mention this to your customer. How can you expect a customer to trust you if you make it obvious that your employer cannot trust you? *It is only the stupid man who tries to be too clever.*

Lead your customer as much as you can. If you drive him, you will probably drive him into a corner and he will feel trapped. This will increase sales resistance quicker than anything else. Let the customer convince himself that he wants your lines. Plant ideas and let him see the point for himself. Argue as little as possible. Be reasonable in what you say in the first place and you may find there will be nothing to argue about.

Make your selling professional. There are too many amateurs on the road. If your selling is truly professional you will reap the professional rewards. Be professional in every way; the way you dress, the way you talk, by understanding your product, by knowing in advance all the answers to all the questions you may be asked.

Be relaxed and congenial in your attitude, especially in the face of criticism or complaint. Remember that no firm can ever hope to please all their customers all the time. Things are bound to go wrong. Errors will occur. Deliveries will be delayed. See the customers point of view. Understand your firm's point of view. Bring the two as near together as you can. Be reasonable, and call for reasonableness from the customer. Remember that an explanation is better than an excuse.

A further aspect of professional selling is the use of words. Use the words which call for an order such as *new* or *up-to-the-minute, special, fashionable*. Induce your customer to see that if he buys from you he can be a leader of fashion. Say you as much as you can and I as little as possible. Make your conversation about your goods interesting. Talk of processes and how they were discovered. Impress the prospect with the fact that your firm is go-ahead, looking always for the latest and best and offering it before anyone else.

Where it is possible stress the value of the dealer placing his orders with one firm, especially if in return you can offer him sole agency in his district. Point out the advantages of this to him, saying the bargain must benefit both parties. If he will buy only from you, you in turn will sell only to him providing his orders are reasonable. Tell him he can sell more if he has the lines exclusively. This way you may well sell more also, and with less effort.

Selling professionally benefits your employer in so far as there are always fewer returns and fewer complaints or misunderstandings when a salesman has done his job honestly and well. Make your trading terms clear to the customer so that there is no possibility of misunderstanding at any time. Do not take orders on promises your firm cannot keep. Do not offer sale or return or exchange terms to get an order when you know very well this is against the company policy. Never mislead the customer to get an order. Remember *goods supplied on false premises are not sold at all*.

Find your main selling angle, be it price, or exclusiveness, or advertising, and whatever it is plug it for all you are worth. Keep on creating confidence in the goods you offer for sale. You must have observed the value of repetition. The most successful companies plug their main selling themes over and over again. You remember 'Heineken refreshes the parts that other beers cannot reach.' You may even remember 'OXO gives a meal man appeal' and 'You're never alone with a Strand.' Slogans are repeated over and over again. It pays. It must pay, because the more successful the company the more repetition in their advertising. Make up your mind what your main selling theme is and plug it. For lines at different price levels I have successfully used the same slogan for years. One of these was 'If you buy from me you can compete with anybody.' A simple statement that was sent out on every catalogue, every sales letter for years. If you say it often enough it sinks in, is remembered, and it is believed more often than not.

Simplicity is golden. Use the simple approach. Do not be over technical. Talk at the right level always. Talk to be understood. Repeat yourself to be remembered. Speak only the truth to be believed.

In your approach *give the impression you are worth seeing.* Do not appear to be on a hit-or-miss tour. Be expectant. People respond to the man who seems very sure of himself; who gives the impression of knowing he has something worthwhile to show or to talk about. Why should the prospect be interested if you are not? Get rid of the hang-dog expression. Look successful. Speak authoritatively. Radiate confidence with every word and gesture.

When having difficulty influencing a prospect to stock your goods, use the following approach which I have found most effective. For the sake of the illustration let us again assume you are selling costume jewellery. The prospect wonders if he can sell the line. Ask the prospect how many of his customers wear costume jewellery. Point to the people passing the shop. Point out the woman wearing a necklet, the other with two brooches, the one with ear-rings, and so on. Then say that all these people must buy these goods somewhere and they all walk past your shop. Say it would be a good idea to stop them!

It is important that you know all about the lines you sell, but if you are asked something and you do not know the answer, say so. Then go and get the answer so that you can answer the question next time.

Many salesmen are totally stumped by the customer who says, 'I don't want anything. Look at all that stock I've got.'

If in response to this you say you will call another time, the probability is that before your next call someone will get the order. What can you say to get an order there and then in the face of the stock position presented to you? Firstly, you must congratulate the customer by saying he must be well known in the town for his varied stock. Then say he will wish to maintain this reputation by always adding the very latest items to come on the market, even if he only buys a few in order to be up-to-date in his window display. This way you may get your case open, and once buying, the customer will no doubt buy more than he intended.

I once read a book on salesmanship from which a certain snappy sentence made a great impression on me. The statement was: 'Never be thankful for small mercies.' This has remained with me long after I have forgotten who wrote it. Make a note of it. Always expect to sell big. Never give the impression you will be satisfied with a small order or you will probably get one.

A vexed question over which there is much argument among salesmen and sales managers is the problem as to whether it is better to undersell or oversell. Let me say at once that *many a salesman who says he does not believe in overselling is only making an excuse for not selling enough,* but let us consider this question more fully. One indisputable fact is this: stock not shown is not sold. If you sell a little to a retailer it is more likely that it will not be shown, and when you next call he will say:

'See, I only bought a little, and I've still got it.'

You say, 'Where is it?'

He replies, 'Right here, under the counter,' or 'In this drawer.' He further says, 'If I cannot sell the little bit I bought I obviously don't want any more.'

The position is, he was sold a little so he did not worry about it. When considering display, his stock of the particular line was too small to merit space.

To undersell is often to lose a customer.

Suppose you oversell. The goods arrive. The buyer is a bit startled at the amount he bought, and he says to his assistant:

'Make some room in the window, I must show this lot or I'll never sell it all.'

A good display leads to good sales and when the salesman calls again the customer is delighted and places another order.

'Damn good selling stuff, yours,' he says. 'It's sold like hot cakes!'

It sold because it was shown.

I am firmly convinced that to undersell is to lose display prominence and possibly to lose a customer. To oversell is to get prominent display and repeat orders. Shops throughout the country are littered with odds and ends of this or that the buyer tried a little of, and never sold. *Sell enough to merit good display* and your sales will increase and your repeat business will be steady, and regular.

Part of the art of good salesmanship lies in the ability of the salesman to educate the buyer away from the tendency to only buy what he likes. This is important. Skilfully done, it leads to increased business and the gratitude of the buyer.

A very important tip that I think essential to successful salesmanship – each would-be salesman should develop his own personality and not aspire to copy someone else. Go ahead and develop your own natural ability.

Now lets think back on some of the important things to come out of this chapter:

- Be sincerely interested in the customer and his business.

- You cannot demand loyalty, you have to earn it.

- It pays to make friends in business.

- Be aggressively friendly.

- It is not enough to make friends – you must also influence them.

- Goodwill cannot easily be destroyed.

- Make your statements believable – and don't tell lies.

- Remember a friendly atmosphere is restful, which is good for taking orders.

- The complete salesman can build confidence in other people.

- Make your call on your customer a pleasure for both of you.
- Do not put up with rudeness and condescension on the part of the buyer – remember you are equals.
- The salesman and the buyer need each other.
- Never waste a buyers' time.
- Persevere. Get that first order, then get another.
- There are no bad months, only bad customer relationships.
- Show the buyer how much he will make by selling your goods.
- Time spent in your car is time when you are not earning.
- Remember an explanation is better than an excuse.
- Goods not shown are goods not sold.
- Sell enough to merit good display.

18

SKILL ON THE ROAD

In any profession it is of the utmost importance that all facets of the job should be fully mastered. Yet, there are commercial travellers who have never mastered the car. This is absolutely beyond my comprehension.

Many spend their hours in the car being aggressive and fuming at other drivers. In the evening they complain how tired they are with all this driving. The first thing a commercial traveller needs to do well is drive. Yet, like so many other people, many travellers are content just to pass the driving test and then to leave driving improvement right out of their minds. Even books on salesmanship do not as a rule make any mention of this. Why?

Every man making his living on the road should study to master the art of safe, fast driving. He should enjoy driving. He should buy the best car he possibly can. Miles per gallon or litre are far less important than calls per day. Here comes the question of attitude again. Will it be a cheap car, with good economy, or something more powerful that will have smooth acceleration and will get you from call to call quickly and without effort. The right choice of car may easily help you to squeeze in an extra call or two especially in an area where your calls are a good distance apart.

Having the best car possible is no good at all if you cannot handle a car well. No one likes to have their driving criticised but it is a sad fact that many travelling salesmen have accidents that keep them off the road for a while. You cannot sell if you are laid up with your leg in plaster or worse.

If you are a good salesman you will, like me, have to drive in excess of 1000 miles a week, every week. Today you have to exercise great care not to be caught breaking the law on the road. Even minor offences can result in a ban under the totting up procedure. For a salesman who depends on his car so much, to be caught over the drink/drive limit is nothing short of stupidity.

Your attitude to your driving is vitally important if you want to succeed in selling.

19

A WORD OF WARNING

The salesman who finds himself successfully working for someone else soon feels that he would make far more money running a business for himself. If he starts in business for himself as a sales agent or wholesaler carrying stock, as I have suggested already, this is usually quite safe. If, though, he feels that it would be a good idea to be a manufacturer, warehouseman or retailer himself, the road is beset with pitfalls, as I have found out myself.

The point is that a man may be a first class salesman without being a good businessman when it comes to matters of finance and accountancy. This may well result in over optimism or lack of financial control leading to insolvency.

One salesman who went into business for himself and went bankrupt said ruefully that he could not understand the outcome of his business efforts as he was the cheapest in the business and should have made pots of money. He overlooked the elementary fact that enough profit must be made to cover all contingencies or a business is worth nothing, and becomes more insolvent the more it sells.

I can earn myself a first class income at any time selling and organising sales but I am apt to lose money if I try to run a big business.

I would strongly advise any really successful salesman who wants to run his own business to arrange a tie-up with an accountant and a business manager. He, himself, should concentrate on sales and marketing and be advised by his partners as to the use of funds.

If a salesman insists on entering into business on his own, in spite of these comments, let him at least be advised that he must have enough money to finance at least three months' turnover.

Everything considered however, a top salesman should stick to selling. He can earn more money with less risk in his own field than by any other method.

20

SALES CASES

Most of the sales cases illustrated in this chapter are from my own experience. I have learned a good deal over the years, during which I have sold at almost every level, and it is hoped that these illustrations may help the salesman just beginning his sales career to be more able in answering problems, dealing with complaints, and opening new accounts.

CASE 1

A salesman's report reached me to the effect that a certain customer had said he would not deal with us any more as our deliveries were not satisfactory. The salesman said he had made all the excuses he could think of, but could not change the customer's mind. Would I care to go along and see if I could do anything about the matter?

I duly called at the shop concerned and announced myself. The customer said:

'I told your rep I did not want to have anything more to do with your firm.'

'I don't blame you,' I said. 'We're a horrible lot.'

'I didn't say that, not at all,' said the customer.

'Then,' said I, 'How is it you feel as you do about us? What's the trouble? I expect it can be put right in a few minutes.'

'Well,' he said, becoming more agreeable as a result of the way I was speaking to him, 'We never damn well get what we order.'

I produced the customer's last order and said, 'Here's your last order. It was for 107 different lines which come from 11 different countries and 37 different makers. Of the 107 lines, we supplied 81 by return, 20 more have been supplied as available. This leaves exactly 6 which have not been supplied in the eight weeks since you placed the order. Which is 5%, which does not bear out your statement that you never get what you order. You get 75 to 80% by return, and 95% over 6 to 8 weeks. The remaining items are probably being discontinued because they have had a long run, or they have been held up by the latest dock strike, or dropped by us because we think we now have a better line to replace one or the other of them. I wonder if you really consider that a delivery by return of more than 75% of an order is bad service when I tell you that we run 4000 lines. It is not possible to always have all these lines in stock. We buy all over the world and all sorts of delays occur for which we are not responsible at all.' As I said this I moved over to the counter and picked up an article which I knew to be a fast selling line (it was a headscarf with a very beautiful design). 'By the way, while I'm here I badly need four of these. Let me have them, will you.'

The customer said, 'I'm afraid I havn't got four, sir.'

'Why not?' I said, 'Can't I get what I order from you? Not more than 25% of what I ask for? This is a good line and you must know it. Why is it not available from your stock?'

The customer looked a bit sheepish and I laughed out loud. 'Come off it,' I said. 'You get better service from us than you are able to give me.'

The man thought of every reason why he could not be expected to have four of this scarf in stock. How did he know how many he would sell of this particular line? It was a fast seller and he could not keep it in stock, and so on.

You will see that all his arguments applied equally to us in our inability to supply his order completely, and this he finally accepted, and had to admit that we served him a lot better than he could serve me.

I booked a very good order from him, bought the scarf, reiterated that we were a horrible lot, pumped his hand vigorously, and said, 'I'm ever so glad you didn't have four of those scarves.' We both laughed and have been good friends ever since. As he said to my traveller later, 'That Mr Cole's a rum one.'

CASE 2

This is all about ghost towns. You know the places. Everybody else has good accounts there but you are quite sure the place is dead. Maybe it even smelled dead. So you did not stop. Next time though you made two calls. Nothing doing. The traders seem to be dead too.

The truth is that you might as well be dead.

There is not a town in the country where my firm's goods cannot be sold, and there never will be. After hearing over and over again from a traveller I employed that there were only two towns in one county worth bothering with, I decided to visit this desert land to see if it really was impossible to get business in about sixty small places. I decided to try three of them for a start. I adopted the same procedure in each place, as follows:

I picked the shop I wanted to deal with and entered, told the owner who I was and started to explain the reason for my visit:

I said, 'I don't expect you've ever seen my traveller, but he's been around these parts, and he says everything's dead and the retailers are included in this description. I've had a look around the place, had a nice pot of tea at five past nine just down the road. You cannot do that everywhere. What I really want to know is this: Is it true that nobody here wants to do business? It may be a small place, but it's very nice. I like it. I like your shop. The window is well dressed as though you expected to do business. Now, my company are the very best in the country for costume jewellery. We have the biggest range offering the widest selection. We are not necessarily the cheapest, but we have things that are different, and that's what is usually wanted in a small community. You can't have everybody at the Women's Institute wearing the same necklet, and that's what happens when only the cheapest lines are sold. Forgive me for talking so much, but it's my business to talk and I know what I'm talking about. If you buy from me you will have the most interestingly different range of costume jewellery for miles around. Will you have a look? After all, the proof of the pudding is in the eating, and, in any case, I want to prove to my traveller that he is wrong to think that only the big towns have enterprising retailers,' and so on.

In each place I visited I did business. I wrote and told the traveller for the area that there had been a resurrection of the dead, and that if he used his loaf he could do business anywhere. It's true. *They have not built the place yet where a good salesman cannot sell his goods.*

CASE 3

This is about price conscious buyers. The people who know their limits. The people who live in those places that are not like anywhere else, where everybody is very careful with their money.

These people say to the traveller, 'My limit is £5 cost.' The average salesman therefore shows items costing up to £5 and continues to do so for years. After all, why should anything change or improve? Let well alone.

Here is one illustration from many I could give. After having dealt with a certain lady running a general ladies wear shop for some time, I suggested to her, when Christmas was drawing near, that it would pay her to improve her trade year by year and that the best time to try to do this is at Christmas time. I pointed out that she could probably sell at a pound or two more than she had done before, and that on the odd item she might do even better. I pointed out that cars were dearer, bus fares had gone up, and so on, and that people were conditioned to some extent to pay more for things than a year ago. Also, I pointed out that no doubt she had noticed her customers wearing better lines than she sold. I asked her 'Why don't you sell these things to them instead of working just as hard to sell them something cheaper?'

I showed this good lady a range of items more expensive than she had ever bought. She was delighted with them and said she had no idea we did such nice things. I told her that this was her fault as these numbers were always available and she had refused to believe she could sell anything over a certain price.

The result has been that this customer has built up a much better class trade than she believed possible, and not

94

only in jewellery. She has now branched out in better coats, skirts, etc. Many customers restrict their own sales because of preconceived notions as to what they can sell. They will not move from their point of view until they have complete confidence in the person advising them to do so. Get this confidence and you will sell to the customer what you want to sell.

CASE 4

In a small seaside town on the East Coast I was told that two Cockney ladies had opened a summer season shop, but that they were very tough and suspicious of all salesmen. Now, I believe in approaching people according to the situation. Cockneys, as a rule, do not like what they call the 'toffee-nosed' approach, and these two ladies were real down to earth types, and a bit on the defensive because of their cockney accents. They loved London and I was told that travellers who told them how lucky they were to be able to live now where they could get some fresh air left in a hurry without an order.

I waited outside until there were no customers. I then walked in and said:

'Whatcher, me old cock sparrows.'

Dead silence. Then one of the ladies said 'He's from the smoke.' I did not contradict this. I had lived in London a lot and liked the Cockneys. They were soon all over me, and we talked about London. After about twenty minutes one of them said:

'You on 'oliday here?'

'No,' I said, 'I'm a bloody salesman.'

They both roared with laughter and asked what I sold. From here on it was easy going. I left the shop and brought them in some fish and chips and they made some tea, and in between mouthfuls I took the best order yet taken in that shop. They became good customers and friends of mine.

'Cor, stone the crows, you can sell to anyone if you use a bit of savvy.'

CASE 5

Versatility is essential to salesmanship. Adaptability is worth its weight in gold. In contrast to the case above, I have had to sell to the type of person who would not tolerate a man who swore, to whom a nine o'clock appointment means nine o'clock and not five to or five past. When calling on one of these people, for whom I feel a little sorry, I act in a way which will please them.

'Good morning, sir.'

The buyer returns the greeting. I confirm my appointment. Ask if I may bring my samples in. Ask if he minds if I bring in six cases at once, or would he prefer to look through one range at a time, and not clutter up the shop with my cases. Knowing that the man I am talking to is a creature of habit, I suggest an adjournment for coffee at the appropriate time. I explain in the greatest detail our trading terms, our difficulties, ask his co-operation where necessary, make sure that everything is done properly. You can sell to anyone if you adapt yourself to the type of person you are confronted with. Appreciate them and their point of view. As I said above, I feel sorry for the humourless, meticulous type. I feel that they miss a lot of fun in life, but that is their affair, and I want to earn money from all types.

CASE 6

The following will illustrate the use of praise in salesmanship. I was finding it a bit difficult to sell to a certain male buyer who seemed quite certain that I could not possibly have anything he could not get from the people he already dealt with. I was racking my brain for a way to prove him wrong but felt that it was unlikely that I would do so by argument, and he would not look at anything. So, I said:

'Well, I'm sorry you are not interested in my lines. Before I go however, may I congratulate you on the layout of your shop. It looks very nice indeed. The lighting is terrific and the decor wonderful. You have the setting for showing off the most wonderful lines. In fact, you are making less interesting lines look quite delightful. I can think of some of our lines that would really be shown to advantage here.'

'You like it,' he said, in a quite different voice.

'Oh, yes, it's marvellous,' I said.

He looked at his watch. 'I can give you an hour,' he said, 'Show me some of your best pieces.'

'Certainly,' I said, 'I wouldn't dream of showing you anything else for sale in a shop like this.'

Before I left the buyer was asking my advice as to whether he could improve the shop in any way and I was able to say that I could not see how, but thought he had improved the range of goods he was now going to carry. He said that he was glad he had looked and hoped I would forgive his reluctance, but there were so many travellers all carrying the same stuff. I said that I was pleased he had found the time to look, two hours incidentally, and that I hoped he would be successful with our merchandise as I was sure he would be.

The fact remains, however, that this customer would never have believed I had anything different to show. He would not have looked if I had not praised his shop. A compliment often paves the way to a contract.

CASE 7

Advertising is a sales weapon of the first order. To be able to offer goods that are widely advertised means that one is half way to a sale from the first word. However, there are always some customers who say that advertising does not interest them. I remember a conversation with the owner of a shop on the South Coast in which a wide range of goods were sold. The prospect said to me:

'I do not want to buy from any new firms. Advertising does not mean a thing. A woman comes in here for a necklet. She does not care whether it is advertised or not.'

After looking around, I said, 'I notice you only sell Gillette razor blades. I see you have Pretty Polly tights and Gossard underwear, and that almost everything you have in ladies wear is a brand name.'

The prospect said nothing so I pushed my advantage by pointing out that probably the same thing was said about these items when they first appeared on the market.

Prospects will use all sorts of arguments to avoid placing an order under certain circumstances. The good salesman always has the answer. That is one reason why one man gets his quota of orders every day and another does not.

CASE 8

It is always helpful, in selling to the retailer, to have answers to the retailer's problems which get in the way when they want to stock your lines, for instance the problems of space and display. In my case, selling costume jewellery to shops carrying several hundred other lines already, I run up against this problem rather often. A very large number of my customers have limited space.

A prospect said to me, 'If I buy, where on earth can I show the stuff? I have hardly any space available anywhere.'

I looked around, then said, 'The best way to display costume jewellery is on pegboard. This cuts out the need for display case space, and in any case, costume jewellery does not sell well when put under glass. You could have the sides of your windows covered with pegboard which could give and excellent display. You can also display items on the garments you sell. You can drape necklaces over the handbags in the window. Another good idea is to make a piece of pegboard to hang in the shop door window; this will give you an extra display after hours. Also you can bring this display inside during the day.'

Having shown myself to be interested in his problem the retailer was prepared to take up my products and to try out the methods of display I had suggested. Also he was pleased to be able to use space he did not realise he was not using.

CASE 9

We have already looked at the question of price with regard to the maximum price at which a retailer can sell goods if he

98

tries. There is however, still the question of cost price. There are buyers who make it their main aim in life to sell only lines they can buy at the lowest possible price. This usually means that they are not the retailers with the best range of goods available. However you may wish to deal with them if possible. If so, remember this, it is not always the man with the cheapest article who gets the business. You have to do a big selling job here. Let me illustrate.

I approached a retailer who was obviously only selling the very cheapest merchandise available. Not only was it cheap, it looked cheap. This man was obsessed with the question of price. So, he sold very cheap, and made little profit.

I told him who I was and was told that he had heard of me, and that I was too dear. I said that I could give him a brooch to sell at £2 that looked worth £3 and that I thought this a better deal for him than to be selling for £1 something that looked worth about 50p. I was on dangerous ground here because it is not usually a good thing to criticise a man's buying if you want to sell to him! However this seemed to be the only way to deal with this customer. He said that it was a very cheap neighbourhood and he had to be cheap and admitted that he only earned 25% gross on many lines. I asked if he was successful in selling a gross of each. At this he nearly had a fit. 'Lucky to sell a dozen of anything,' he told me.

I pointed out that if he bought brooches at 40p and sold at 50p and sold a dozen he earned exactly £1.20. On the other hand if he bought only 3 brooches from me at £1 cost and sold at £1.80 he would make £2.40. He would need a quarter of the customers to make twice the profit.

He would have no difficulty in selling our lines at the prices suggested by me because they looked well worth it. I said to the prospect that he must admit that the lines he was buying so cheap looked cheap, whereas we always aimed to sell at a reasonable price items which looked worth much more. To soften the blow, and to make it appear not to come direct from myself to him, I pointed out a saying which I had incorporated into one of our news sheets: 'Any fool can buy rubbish cheap.'

I won the argument and this prospect improved his trade considerably and remained a good customer.

There are several other arguments which can be used in this matter of price. Against cheapness can be set service, variety, continuity of supply, fewer complaints from customers, and so on.

CASE 10

The salesman's time is of great importance and should not be frittered away or spent taking small orders and missing big orders. Consider this conversation with a prospect on whom a special call had been made by request. After the usual introductions the conversation went:

Prospect: 'I only want a little.'

Me: 'How much is a little?'

Prospect: 'Well, I thought of spending about £30.'

Me: 'I have no objection to taking an order for £30 but I cannot show the range for £30. It takes a long time to show our range, or even half of it. I can send one of our selected parcels of the latest lines if you care to indicate the price range you require.'

After some argument this was agreed. I had an order for £30 in fifteen minutes or so instead of after about two hours.

CASE 11

This case arose out of a representative's report that business had dropped considerably in a certain town and that he did not consider that calls in the town were worthwhile in future. I decided to check up on this and found that the representative was quite right. I called on the customers in the town and they were all very down in the mouth. I decided there must be a cause for this and that business must be available somewhere as girls in the town were wearing the latest jewellery. I therefore motored around a bit and found two new estates on the outskirts of the town in both of which I opened new accounts bigger than those we had previously had in the town centre. Representatives should be alive to the changes in a town. Should know about new estates and work on them.

CASE 12

Every salesman hears at some time or another the old battle cry of the reluctant buyer, 'I'm sorry, we cannot open any new accounts.' Whenever this is said to me I am afraid it annoys me very much because it is about the most stupid and inane reason any buyer can give for not looking at your goods. Why on earth can they not open any new accounts? Can they close any bad ones?

A buyer's job is to buy. To buy well it is essential to know what is on offer. For this reason alone any buyer worth the name will consider all goods on offer. Even if he is satisfied with his suppliers surely he can say so instead of trotting out the old chestnut about not opening any new accounts.

The answer I usually give to buyers who say this is that we are very careful where we open accounts ourselves. We like to pick and choose our customers, and we thought the prospect looked to be of the standard to sell our goods and to sell them well, but if this is not possible there are no doubt many firms in the town who will be glad to stock our range. Further I tell them with absolute conviction that if a competitor of theirs stocks our range their own sales will fall. This usually works.

CASE 13

No time. How often do you meet with that answer to your request to show your goods – 'I'm sorry, I havn't time today.'

If a prospect says this to me I usually say that I made the time to call and see them. That I am prepared to wait a while if they are very busy, but surely they have to make time to look at goods which may be of interest to them. That there are two sides to this question of time. The time of the salesman is important too. It must be admitted that one must study one's customers wishes as far as possible, but with a lot of buyers the truth is that they are not busy at all and this is just an excuse. If you are able to say something to whet their appetite they usually make the time to see you. In my own experience I have been told eventually that I can be given half an hour, and have had a job to get away in two hours. In my experience also I would say that the really busy people always have time to consider any worthwhile proposition.

The answer that the buyer has not the time to see you is usually a defence mechanism indulged in to protect the buyer from wasting time. It is the salesman's job to convince the buyer that he is worth seeing, and that time spent looking at his range is as good as money in the bank. Most buyers will make time to see a man if they are convinced that profit will result.

CASE 14

This illustration is borrowed from another source and concerns two shoe salesmen who were sent to a native island to sell shoes. One cabled his firm: 'Natives do not wear shoes, returning home.'

The second salesman cabled his office: 'Natives do not wear shoes. Opportunities tremendous. Hold sample stocks in readiness for demand.'

If you learn the lesson implicit in this story you will be on the way to becoming a successful salesman.

21

FINDING A JOB

Taking it for granted that you have the right approach to life, the right attitude in fact, you have to find a job. If possible, the right job. This is most important.

It can be said, without doubt, that salesmanship is the best paid job in the world if the salesman is prepared to invest as much in his work as others invest in the way of money or training in their business or profession.

This brings me back to the question of attitude again. If you are prepared to put all you have into a job of selling you can become one of the higher paid and more successful members of the community. In no other occupation is it possible to earn such good money so soon. Within a year of starting the real salesman can be earning well over £20000 a year. That is providing he is prepared to accept payment by results. This brings us back to attitude again. You must believe in yourself and be prepared to stand on your own feet. You must then put all you've got into the job of selling. Returning to the first sentence of this chapter, we will presume that your attitude is right, and that you lack only the job.

The alternatives before you are:

[1]   a position as a representative on salary, expenses, and small commission, or

[2]   as an independent agent on the best commission basis you can obtain.

The choice is yours. If you are frightened by [2] then take [1] and join the army of also rans.

Let me not be misunderstood. There are good salesmen working under the first alternative, and some of them become really good, but unless they eventually start business on their own or obtain a position on the board of the company they work for, they are unlikely to reach the top bracket incomes. This may well explain why it is so difficult to obtain good representatives. The good ones refuse to spend their lives working for less than they are worth. If they are good they start their own businesses as agents or in some other sphere. The result is that the also rans are always answering the advertisements for representatives, and an employer is lucky to obtain, occasionally, one of the stars of the selling profession. He will be wise to pay such a man what he is worth or he will not keep him.

It could be said that the alternatives facing the recruit to salesmanship are not only to be found in the matter of payment, but also in the approach to selling. This can be professional or amateur. The professional is the man who studies to succeed in the same way as a doctor or lawyer, who gives his time to making sure he is fully equipped as possible for his calling. The amateur is the man who has heard there is good money to be got from selling but is not willing to put himself out to succeed, or to work long or unusual hours.

The alternative is between the man who will be wholehearted, keeping nothing in reserve, and the man who wants it easy. When attending an interview for a situation it will be apparent what is your attitude.

Firstly, then, you must decide how you will think, what your attitude will be, what you want. *Security first, or opportunity always.* Your decision on these matters will have a bearing on the job you will look for. It is very little use having the right ideas in the wrong job.

If you are seeking security first and foremost you will look for a position with the best established company you can, where there is most chance of reasonable promotion to area manager or sales manager. In certain jobs you will be able to obtain, you will be little more than an order taker with a regular round of calls to make in a small car provided by the company. Your money will be regular and your position secure, and if you really wanted to be a salesman you would be better off dead.

Here again, I do not wish to be misunderstood. There are lots of nice types in these jobs. Decent fellows. Proud to work for a firm nationally famous. But, what a life! If there is inside you just a spark of enthusiasm you will soon lose it. If you want adventure, a feeling of pleasure at an income earned by your own efforts, this is not the job for you.

Occasionally some young man who could be as secure as he could wish either in commerce or in the ministry at home, receives what he describes as a call from God to take the gospel to some far-flung place in the heart of Africa or India. Even if nobody will sponsor him he goes. He will put up with any indignity, suffer any buffeting, because there is a fire burning within him. He could not do otherwise. C. T. Studd once said he did not 'give a damn or a twopenny toss for anything but Christ and his blood-stained cross'. This is the spirit that is so lacking in the world today. This is the spirit of true salesmanship. After all, preaching the gospel in the wilds without salary or security of any kind is a form of salesmanship. It is the selling of a belief, a faith, not for money but for inner satisfaction or for love of God or one's fellow beings whatever their colour.

Where are the young men of today with the spark that makes the real pioneer, the real missionary, the real salesman? We have so much social security that the average man believes he is entitled to a living as a matter of right. *From the cradle to the grave our people are being molly-coddled into indolence. Enterprise is becoming a dirty word. Every man wants his rights, and cluttered up with National Health teeth and spectacles there are few who will take a bite at any project of daring or who can see an opportunity when it stares them in the face.*

I am afraid I shall be accused of riding a hobby horse. I am a believer in enterprise. I like the man who can stand on his own feet, who will feed his own children, pay his own bills, and earn his own living on his merits. On humanitarian grounds it may be necessary to maintain the useless but need we join them? If there are people who want to have six children when they can only afford two I suppose somebody must look after the children but why in God's name encourage the idiot parents?

I could no more work for a salary than live without water. I like to be paid for what I achieve. I am prepared to starve if I prove unable to merit a good income. I am fully prepared to stand or fall by the results I achieve. Are you?

Whichever attitude you decide to take, whichever kind of job you are going to seek, there are certain principles and attitudes which should be adopted at the time of an interview for any situation.

Firstly, it is important to decide where you wish to work. It may be that you are prepared to work anywhere. On the other hand this may not be possible. Make certain that you are quite clear as to what you want to do as far as the area in which you wish to work is concerned. Be decided about this before you attend an interview.

In this connection it should be said that the matter of area needs considerable thought. It is generally believed that the heavily populated areas are best to work in but I wish to put forward the view that this is not necessarily so.

In a heavily populated area like London, Birmingham, Manchester, etc, the competition for business is most severe. In the less populated areas like the eastern counties competition is far less. When I commenced the sales campaign for a firm which became one of the three largest in its particular trade in four years, I started first with the eastern counties, the lesser travelled home counties, South Wales and Northern Ireland.

I would say that if you are going to sell costume jewellery, handbags, fancy goods, dog collars or any other of the non-technical and non-provision lines, you may well find that you will achieve more quickly the results you wish in a less populated area.

The reason I plumped for the eastern counties was that I was told it was the traveller's graveyard. It seemed to me that if most of the travellers in the area were dead ones it provided me with considerable opportunity to make a good living. It appeared that everybody looked down on South Wales. The general attitude was that apart from Cardiff and Swansea the area was not worth covering, but I found the traders in the valleys were thirsty for goods. The same applies to Northern Ireland and the smaller home counties.

Think seriously therefore regarding the area you wish to cover. Take into account the cost of covering the area, the amount of competition you will encounter from perhaps bigger and better firms, the kind of reception you will be likely to meet.

Remember too, if you are selling a luxury article, that the same kind of article may be offered cheaper on market stalls in the big centres. That in the big centres there will be several local wholesalers competing for the business.

Against this, of course, in a widely dispersed area you will have more travelling to do, fewer customers in a given number of miles, and so on. Weigh the pros and cons carefully. Do not go out at once for what looks like the best area – think about the different areas in relation to the different conditions you will meet.

You may like to bear in mind that it is easier to obtain the kind of job you want in a less popular area. Advertisements in the *Daily Telegraph* for representatives or agents bring more replies from London, Lancs and Yorks than for all the rest of the country put together. Everybody seems to want what looks to be the best area. I will wager however that more representatives lose their jobs in these 'good' areas than in the seemingly less interesting areas.

Another point to consider in these days is that of parking your car. Work in the big cities and suffer. Work in the country areas and you are able to park right by your call. Not only will you find the parking easier but the driving also.

There is also the question of appointments. In country districts these are much easier to obtain and often are not necessary at all. When I was selling books I can remember waiting in a queue of travellers in a West End store for the whole morning without getting to the buyer. Give me the country areas and the much freer attitude one finds there.

There is the question of strikes. These hit the cities and big centres of population first. The country areas are usually free of such disturbances.

In other chapters of this book the need to make friends of your customers has been stressed. This is far easier in the country areas. Country customers are far more loyal. Competitors try to take my customers away from me – but not once have they been successful in any country area.

If you have a big range of goods to show and you show

such a range in the country areas, this is much appreciated as it does not usually happen. In cities the buyers seldom have time to look at a wide range.

Think this out for yourself. Money can be made in all areas.

When attending an interview be free and easy. I am never impressed by an applicant who is over nervous and hesitant. I want to employ men of confidence and adaptability. Not men who are frightened to have any opinions or who are overawed in the presence of a businessman. Do not make the mistake of thinking that you must be very serious. Be natural. Do not pretend to know things you do not know or claim to be able to do anything you are unsure about. Do not hesitate however to state what you believe you can do and be.

Find out from your prospective employer just what backing you will get in the job by way of advertising, good delivery service, enquiries passed to you, etc. Do not for one moment consider working for any employer who says he does not believe in advertising or one who will not pass on all enquiries from your territory. If it is lacking, refuse the job.

Do not necessarily try to work for a very big firm or you may find your opportunities for promotion are very limited. Try to work for an up-and-coming firm with ideas. Look for the kind of employer who is looking for the kind of salesman you intend to be. Try to secure a position which will give you what you are worth. Many very big firms only need order takers and why should they pay you very much?

When intending to appear for an interview do not ask in advance if your expenses to the interview will be paid. Among the few hundred salesmen I have employed I can honestly say that not a single one who asked this question ever turned out to be any good at his job. It follows quite naturally that this should be the case. The security conscious do not make the best salesmen. *The man who is worried about spending three pounds to try to obtain the position he wants will probably be just as worried every time he has to put fuel in his car to call on a customer.* This type of man cannot be a successful salesman. Never.

When attending an interview show enthusiasm for the job of selling. Strain at the leash to get started. Show that this is what you want to do. Do not apologise for enthusiasm. Without it you will never succeed.

In seeking a position, therefore, it is important that you should:

- Decide what you want.

- Know where you want to work.

- Think about how you want to be paid.

- Show enthusiasm for the job.

A salesman without enthusiasm will be a salesman full of complaints and empty of orders.

22

IN CONCLUSION

FAITH

'In quietness and confidence shall be your strength.'
The Bible

Quietness does not mean idleness. The really confident man does not need to bluster. Confidence begets a relaxed attitude. There really is strength in a quietly confident attitude and without this the salesman is considerably handicapped.

The man who is really confident will produce confidence in his customers. A man who cannot believe in what he has to sell should stop trying to sell it.

'Our cheerful faith in all that we behold is full of blessing.'
Wordsworth

I have never been able to understand the salesman who is not cheerful. Why on earth should anyone welcome a sourpuss? I never do. Some salesmen spend most of their time complaining about the weight of their samples, the attitude of the firm they work for, and so on. They air these grievances in front of customers. They look and act sour, and their unfortunate customers are glad to see the back of them.

The man with the faith that is essential to first class salesmanship is bound to be cheerful. Why not? He has every reason to be cheerful. After all, he knows and loves his job, and from it he earns a top class income. The sour man is usually the sour grapes man.

'Faith is the substance of things hoped for.
The evidence of things not seen.'
The Bible

The salesman with faith already has the success he is working for. His state of mind allows only for success. He does not believe in failure. While others are only wondering if a thing can be done, he is already counting not the cost but the results. This is what faith means. Hope is not faith. Faith knows. The man with faith is the successful man. The man with hope may or may not be. The hopeful salesman is always waiting for better days. The man with faith has good days all the time.

'If ye have faith as a grain of mustard seed, ye shall say onto
this mountain, Remove hence to yonder place,
and it shall remove.'
The Bible

You must not believe everything you read or everything you hear, but you can believe the intention of the above biblical verse. The salesman who makes good is the man who knows he can do what is asked of him. It may look impossible to other men but faith can move mountains, and move them faster than anything else.

No coward soul is mine,
No trembler in the world's storm-troubled sphere:
I see heavens glories shine,
And faith shines equal, arming me from fear.
Emily Bronte

At the time of taking on any new job most people suffer an attack of nerves. This is nothing to be ashamed of. Have faith, and faith will overcome these fears. The fearful salesman who lacks confidence cannot hope to succeed. The first setback will only increase the fear. The man of faith will see ahead of him the goal he knows he can attain and will shrug off an early failure as a duck sheds water. When a man faces early disappointment 'He must gather his faith together, and his strength make stronger', as advised by Robert Bridges. In a contest between fear and a faith, a strong faith will always win.

> If thou canst Death defy,
> If thy faith is entire,
> Press onward, for thine eyes
> Shall see thy heart's desire.
> *Robert Bridges*

Men of faith have accomplished almost everything despite difficulties. Henry Ford did not make his first car without problems. He had many problems but his faith was bigger than any of them.

Faith sees beyond the horizon. Faith sees through the barriers. Faith is certain of the result desired. A man can accomplish what he will if he will believe.

> 'Unfaith in aught is want of faith in all.'
> *Tennyson*

Faith by its very nature is consistent. The man who claims to believe today, but doubts tomorrow does not have true faith. The man of faith produces consistent results. The top salesman sells consistently for this reason. The man who is up and down, seemingly wonderful one month and utterly useless the next, is not one of the top salesmen. One of the hallmarks of the top-money salesman is the regularity with which he brings home the bacon.

Faith is honest. As Shakespeare said, 'There are no tricks in plain and simple faith', and the salesman who has faith does not need lies or tricks by which to accomplish his ends. His sales are all honestly made. This leads to a consideration of lies.

LIES

> 'Don't deal in lies.'
> *Rudyard Kipling*

The successful salesman is an honest man. You may hear of the salesman who by tricks and subterfuge books business, but never worry about this. You will still be booking consistent business when such salesmen have lost all their customers. Faith does not need to cheat to accomplish.

Oliver Cromwell said, 'A few honest men are better than numbers.' This is true. I would rather have three men of faith and cheerfulness, who deal honestly with their prospects, than a whole army of liars who can only sell by false pretences.

DILIGENCE

'Diligence is the mother of good fortune
and idleness, its opposite,
never brought a man to the goal of his best wishes.'
Miguel de Cervantes

The super salesman is a diligent man. He works every minute in which it is possible to do business. He has drive. He rests only when he cannot work. He is never idle. This is the price you must pay for success as a salesman. You must be diligent. Damn the boys. To hell with the drink. Who cares if the races are on? Nothing matters like success. Success is shy of the idle.

It is possible for you to be an average man if this is what you want to be, and this you can accomplish without too much diligence. You can bargain for the rate for the job, and then do only as much as you need. You will probably be known as a very nice fellow, never too pressing, a comfortable type, always willing to have drink with the boys, no side about this chap.

However if you want to reach the top in selling you must be diligent. You may not have time for a drink with the boys. It may be that you will not even know the name of the favourite in the Derby. Your time may well be spoken for.

The prize won by the diligent is very high. It is up to you to decide whether you want the prize or not.

ENTHUSIASM

'Nothing was ever achieved without enthusiasm.'
Emerson

It is little good goading yourself to be diligent if you have no enthusiasm for the job you are doing. As Emerson remarks, enthusiasm is the driving force behind worthwhile accomplishments in the world. A man without enthusiasm is like a dud joke – nobody is interested. If you wish to produce interest in the product you have for sale, for heaven's sake show some enthusiasm for it yourself. Your enthusiasm for your work should be an all-compelling drive, a burning fire within you that shows in the way you talk, the way you handle your products, the approach to the prospect. Enthusiasm is the key that opens the door to many a buyer's interest.

> 'Enthusiasm moves the world.'
> *Arthur James Balfour*

Many a tipster owes the success of his trade to the fact that he showed enthusiasm for his fancies. You may find yourself going to see a play that someone else has been very enthusiastic about. If you have asked a friend what the show was like and he says in an off-hand manner, 'Oh, all right,' you may well decide to miss it. The prospect approached by two salesmen is most likely to place his order with the man who showed the most enthusiasm for his work and his prospects.

Another very interesting remark of Emerson's is to the effect that 'We boil at different degrees.' Perhaps this explains why some men achieve so much more than others. There are degrees of faith and degrees of enthusiasm. The most successful salesman is the man with the greater degree of faith and enthusiasm who applies himself diligently to his work, who does not need to cheat to sell.

If I may be permitted again to draw from the wisdom of Emerson, 'People wish to be settled: Only so far as they are unsettled is there any hope for them.'

Spenser refers to the 'Sacred hunger of ambitious minds.' The enthusiastic and ambitious man is the man who finds success within his grasp. You must be ambitious to reach the top. So ambitious that nothing is allowed to stand in your way.

> 'To burn always with this hard, gemlike flame,
> to maintain this ecstacy, is success in life.'
> *Walter Horatio Pater*

I have quoted from so many authorities on life in order to show that my ideas on salesmanship are supported by many writers whose words have been an inspiration to many over the years.

To be really doing the job one wants to, does mean ecstacy. To have the kind of enthusiasm which produces the top results means that a fire does burn within the salesman. This fire is indestructible, the ecstacy experienced betters any pleasure in the world. If you lack this zeal you will never reach the top in selling.

Even the bible tells us that God himself dislikes the lukewarm, as follows, in the book of Revelation: 'Because thou art lukewarm I will spew thee out of my mouth.' Abraham Cowley said, 'Lukewarmness I count a sin.'

In every walk of life the enthusiastic make the greatest impression. The salesman who is not prepared to give all his time and all his energy to the job of selling is lukewarm and will not hit the jackpot.

There is no substitute for enthusiasm.

MAKING FRIENDS

We have said earlier that other things being equal a customer will give his order to the salesman he like most. It is important that the man who would be a successful salesman should like people, and study to make friends. To return again to Emerson, who always seems to hit the nail on the head:

He who has a thousand friends has not a friend to spare,
And he who has one enemy will meet him everywhere.

A man who cannot make friends will never make customers, or if he does, they will be the wrong kind. The successful salesman finishes up selling only to his friends.

DESERVE SUCCESS

Sir Winston Churchill once said, 'No one can guarantee success in war, but only deserve it.'

The salesmen who fail often complain, feeling apparently that they ought to have been successful. This cannot be so. The salesman who deserves to succeed, does succeed. To deserve success means to work for it.

KNOWLEDGE

> 'Knowledge itself is power.'
> *Francis Bacon*

It is essential to success in salesmanship to have a thorough knowledge of one's product, and an equally thorough and perceptive knowledge of people.

A salesman is made up of many parts of which knowledge is one. Some men make the mistake of thinking that knowledge alone will make a salesman. That is why many knowledgeable men fail to become good salesmen. Faith, confidence, sincerity, friendliness, enthusiasm, diligence, all are essential to success. Samuel Johnson, in one sentence, showed his perception as follows:

> 'Integrity without knowledge is weak and useless,
> and knowledge without integrity is
> dangerous and dreadful.'

The reader who would make a success of selling should remember that all the assets of a good salesman are essential to him. To have some and lack the others is not enough. In any profession a man must study to be completely able.

OPPORTUNITY

> 'A wise man will make more opportunities than he finds.'
> *Bacon*

This thought brings us back to the necessity for enthusiasm. An enthusiastic man finds the opportunities he needs. If they are not on the surface he makes them appear. A good salesman creates his opportunities. The salesman who writes to his office complaining that there are no openings for his goods has the wrong job.

WORK

> 'Blessed is he who has found his work,
> let him ask no other blessedness.'
> *Carlyle*

Do you feel like that about your work? If not, you are doing the wrong work. If not, and your work is selling, you will never be a worthwhile salesman.

Do you work because you must, and are you glad when work is over? If so, success in selling is not for you. For me, the days pass all too quickly. I thoroughly enjoy my work.

The top salesman is a very happy man. Not only because of the money he earns but because he is doing the work he loves.

TIME

There is nothing more important in the salesman's life than his use of time. I hope the reader will forgive me for appending here a whole list of quotations about time. The subject is so important that the remarks of thinking men on the matter are worth reading and re-reading.

> 'Dost thou love life? Then do not surrender time, for that's
> the stuff life is made of.'
> 'He that lives upon hope will die fasting.'
> 'Time is money.'
> *Benjamin Franklyn*

> If you can fill the unforgiving minute
> With sixty seconds worth of distance run
> Yours is the earth and everything that's in it.
> *Rudyard Kipling*

SUCCESSFUL SELLING

'No time like the present.'
Mary de la Reviere Manley

'Well,' said the Red Jacket (to someone complaining
that he had not enough time)
'I suppose you have all there is.'
Emerson

How pleasant it is, at the end of the day,
No follies to have to repent;
But reflect on the past, and be able to say,
That my time has been properly spent.
Jane Taylor

Gather your rosebuds while you may,
Old Time is still a-flying:
And this same flower that smiles to-day
To-morrow will be dying.
Robert Herrick

The salesman can never recover tomorrow what he loses today. It is impossible. Every minute wasted is a crime against his occupation and a reason why he is not made of the stuff of which super salesmen are made.

Ask yourself every evening, have I used my time as well as I could? Have I missed an opportunity? Have I been enthusiastic enough in my job to wish to turn every passing second into an entry in my order book?

Time is money. *Time lost is money lost. Time wasted is money wasted.* Would you throw £20 away in the street? No! Then how is it you throw an hour away? In an hour you can earn £20 or more.

A fool and his money are soon parted, we are told. A fool wastes his time and loses the money he might have.

Use every minute as though it were your last. Let nobody waste your time, not even customers. Don't criticise your wife for spending £11.99 on a blouse and then go and throw away £20 worth of time!

The truly busy man is the man who has learnt how to make every minute worth something to him. Not the man who is bustling about getting nowhere at all and having another cup of tea.

The man who makes time his servant makes success his right.

SECURITY

This matter of security is so important that I have left it until last in this chapter. A man's attitude to security can pull him down to a level from which he cannot rise lest he lose his security. To quote Shakespeare:

'Security is mortal's chiefest enemy.'

I have said so much already on this subject that I hesitate to say much more. Were it not so vital I would leave it alone, but I see so much security that it makes me sick at heart.

The man who breaks down trade barriers, opens up new markets, blazes new trails is not security minded. If he was he would stay at home.

Can I postulate that it is agreed the top salesmen are the few among salesmen and that the average and below are the majority? If this is accepted, can I then point out that the majority are security minded? This attitude and mediocrity go together. A man with the faith, the ambition, the zeal which go to make a super salesman does not worry his head about security. He probably never gave it a thought.

I know mediocre salesmen who are prepared to work a territory in return for a car allowance, a basic payment and a small commission. I have employed them. They never produce the figures they should. I tell them that their results are no good. They want to keep the job. I say, on commission only, they can. Oh, no! They are perfectly prepared to be paid to be failures, but they could never stand on their own feet. They have responsibilities, children, a mortgage, etc. and they feel that the world owes them a living. After all, they make the calls. Somebody should pay for the petrol.

What I want to know is this – *why should people be paid to be failures?* Why should security be given to a man who cannot earn it? Why should a business nurse these parasites? Why?

On the other hand the man who has the qualities of the top salesman does not concern himself with security, only with opportunity, and believe me the opportunities for selling today are better than they ever were, and the man who can sell should work for commission only. This way he will earn what he is worth. He will never do so on any other basis. Security is a myth. Suppose you get a job on a comfortable basis. Are you good at it? Then you could earn more on a commission basis. Are you bad at it? Then you lose the job.

The man who would reach the top must be self-reliant. He must be able to work as hard as he can. Not be feeling that he is secure anyway and that's enough for today.

The opportunities are there begging for the men of the right calibre to grasp them. You could be one of them.